Wannabe

Wannabe

CHOOSE YOUR OWN CELEBRITY ADVENTURE

TESSA CLAYTON

JOHN BLAKE

Published by John Blake Publishing Ltd,
3 Bramber Court, 2 Bramber Road,
London W14 9PB, England

www.johnblakepublishing.co.uk

www.facebook.com/johnblakebooks ⓕ
twitter.com/jblakebooks ⓣ

This edition published in 2015

ISBN: 978 1 78418 331 8

British Library Cataloguing-in-Publication Data:

A catalogue record for this book is available from the British Library.

Design by www.envydesign.co.uk

Printed in Great Britain by CPI Group (UK) Ltd

1 3 5 7 9 10 8 6 4 2

Papers used by John Blake Publishing are natural, recyclable products made
from wood grown in sustainable forests. The manufacturing processes
conform to the environmental regulations of the country of origin.

Every attempt has been made to contact the relevant copyright-holders,
but some were unobtainable. We would be grateful if the
appropriate people could contact us.

WARNING!

This book contains sex, nudity and stupidity. In that respect, it is like any other celebrity memoir. However, inside this bright pink tome you have the opportunity to determine your own fate as you seek to become the UK's latest diva. There are decisions to be made throughout, and your choices will affect the course of your adventure. Will you find the stardom such a talented and beautiful young woman deserves? Or will you just end up another failed wannabe? You decide.

1

You were born at Queen's Hospital in Romford, on 25 February 1990.

'Congratulations, it's an Essex girl!' announced the midwife, scooping up the false eyelashes and bottle of fake tan that had popped out with the afterbirth.

Your parents had only been together for a matter of months, but they were delighted to have you. Your mum was Miss Chingford 1988, and you inherited her blue-grey eyes and wavy golden hair. Your dad – Tommy 'Dodger' Sullivan – was a used-car dealer, and you got his sense of honesty and fair play.

They called you Shampayne, after their favourite drink – spelt the English way, though, because they hated the French almost as much as they hated Labour supporters, immigrants, homosexuals, Scottish people, feminists and benefits scroungers.

The name suited you: bubbly and full of fizz, you were great to have at parties, and at your best with smoked salmon. In fact, you were good with any type of fish. Aquatic creatures were your passion; you'd spend hours watching the Koi carp that lived in the pond at the bottom of the garden, as they twisted and turned in the murky depths. You begged and begged for your own pet goldfish, Swimmy, and now he slept beside you at night in a glass of water. Somehow you felt a deep spiritual connection with these small-brained, cold-blooded organisms, a bond that was to last a lifetime.

Right from the start, Mum made sure you made the best of yourself. Sometimes it was hard – you weren't allowed to play in the sandpit because you might break a nail, and it was almost impossible climbing trees in high-heeled wedges – but you knew she had your best interests at heart.

'You're going to make something of yourself, Shampayne,' she'd tell you at bedtime, as she read to you from the Argos catalogue. 'You've got beauty *and* lack of brains – the full package.'

Your early days in Essex were some of the happiest of your life. You were a joyful, carefree, perma-tanned child, who loved nothing better than frolicking on the escalators at Bluewater Shopping Centre, or playing at your mum's feet as she got a Brazilian wax. Little did you know that the idyll was about to end.

You'd just turned five when Mum and Dad went on holiday without you to Bali. Nana Rose, your mum's mum, came down from the East End to look after you. She was grateful for the company, as she'd been alone – unless you count Satan, her Staffie – since Grandad had 'gone to Belmarsh'. You guessed Belmarsh must be another word for Heaven seeing as no one had seen him since 1985.

But after Mum and Dad had been gone a month, Nana Rose sat you down for a talk.

'Your mum and dad are having such a lovely time out in Bali that they're going to be staying for a bit,' she told you.

Your little face crumpled at once; mascara ran down your cheeks in rivers.

'How long will they be gone, Nana?'

'Eight to 12 years for your mum, your dad might stay for 20,' she told you. 'It depends on good behaviour.'

'So if I'm really, really good, they'll come back sooner?'

'No, silly...' Nana Rose clasped you to her 36FF surgically enhanced bosom; there was a hiss as a little bit of air escaped. 'You're going to live with me instead,' she explained. 'But we can't stay here in Essex. Your dad says we should lie low for a while.'

You perk up at that. Lilo-ing sounds like fun. 'Will we be living by the beach, Nana?' you ask hopefully.

'I wish,' she sighs. 'No, it's much worse than that. We're going to... *The Countryside.*'

The Countryside is a grey, run-down, miserable place. But to a child used to the shopping malls and beauty salons of Essex, it's hell. There's nothing to see for miles around except trees and birds, meadows, gamboling lambs, waterfalls and flowers. Most of the time it's too muddy for stilettos, so you have to stay in, and the whole place stinks of poo.

You'd hoped you might make friends, but while the boys seem quite friendly, the girls tease you for being different. 'Why do you always carry a dog in your bag?' they ask you, when they spot Satan's head sticking out of your school rucksack. 'It's cruel to keep it in there all day.'

Wannabe

It isn't entirely their fault; they've never met anyone from Essex before, and they don't understand your culture. But the teachers have no excuse. Some of them are openly racist. 'Shampayne Sullivan, why are you as brown as my dining table?' shouts the Headmistress as you come into school late after a sunbed session.

At night you cry yourself to sleep. Why has your life turned out like this? You remember Mum's tender words: 'You're gonna go places, Shampayne! Be the best, and fuck the rest!', and the tears flow even harder.

One night, Nana Rose comes in and sits on your bed. 'Right, name some names,' she rasps. 'Nana Rose will sort things out once and for all.'

Still sobbing, you tell Nana about the racist teachers, and horrible girls, and how they're making your life a misery.

'Leave it with me,' says Nana Rose, cracking her knuckles. 'I'll make a few phone calls.'

And whatever Nana Rose does, it works! Almost overnight, the teachers get off your case, and the girls in the playground are hauled away by their parents whenever they see you coming.

From then on, life in The Countryside gets better. And it gets better still once puberty hits. Almost overnight, you blossom from a flat-chested duckling into a swan with ginormous knockers. It seems men can't take their eyes off you. 'She's good enough to eat,' you hear them mutter, and it's true. Your buttocks are as pert as peaches, your tummy is flat as a pancake and your breasts are like ripe melons. Unfortunately, your foo-foo resembles a Ginsters Chicken & Bacon pasty, although it's nothing that minor surgery can't fix.

Your one regret is that you still don't have any female friends.

Wannabe

You're not sure why, but other girls don't seem to warm to you. You've tried getting off with their boyfriends so you've got something in common to talk about, but nothing seems to win them over. They're obviously just well jel of your star quality and stunning good looks.

'Shampayne Sullivan will do anything for 20p' graffiti starts to appear on park benches and pub walls around town. Well, if your mum taught you anything, it's how to market yourself.

Life's bearable at last, but what you long for more than anything is a soulmate. Someone who can really get to know the real you, which is buried under a thick layer of fake you, then another layer of superficial you, and an extra-deep layer of phoney you. Someone who can discover the peanut kernel underneath all that, that is your soul. It probably needs to be someone with a microscope.

And then you meet Dean. He doesn't have a microscope, either literally or metaphorically, but he does have a van. And when the nearest nail bar is over 30 miles away, that makes him pretty hot stuff.

'I've noticed you coming out of school,' he says, pulling up beside you in his battered Ford Transit. 'Do you fancy a ride?'

You give Dean the once-over. He's just the way you like your men: spikey-haired, weasel-faced and smelling of cheap deodorant. And driving a van.

'Sure, why not?' You hop in beside him. 'How fast can this thing go?'

'Wait and see,' he smiles, putting the van into first gear. You zoom off down the road at 30mph, the bodywork shaking and the engine making uncomfortable screeching noises; the wind rushes in through the hole in the windscreen and tousles your hair extensions. You feel so alive, so exhilarated! Dean pulls out into the outside lane to overtake an old lady in a Nissan Micra, and you feel a little thrill run through your body.

'What's happening to me?' you wonder. 'Could this be first love?'

An hour later you're in the back of the van, face down, as Dean gives it to you on a pile of old towels. You can't believe things are moving so fast – usually you wait at least *two* hours – but it feels so right. Dean's tuned the radio to Heart FM, and it smells like he's sprayed the towels with Febreze. You really think this guy could be The One.

When it's over, you lie nestled in Dean's arms, talking about your hopes and dreams.

'I'm not going to stay in The Countryside all my life,' you tell him. 'I want to be famous.'

'My cousin wanted to be famous,' Dean says.

'What happened?' you ask. '*Is* he famous?'

'Nah,' says Dean. 'He works at the Chunky's Chicken factory.'

Dean pulls you closer. 'Why would you want to leave here anyway?' he says. 'We're together now, and that's what matters.'

You press your body against his. 'Dean,' you say, 'I know I've only just met you, but I feel you've delved inside me like no one has ever delved before. You've seen places deep inside that I've never let anyone else see.'

That seems to get Dean going again and before you know it, you're making passionate love once more. It's six, maybe seven minutes you'll never forget.

At first Dean seems like the perfect boyfriend; you spend every free moment together. But pretty soon, you realise he has issues.

First off, he has a problem with the way you dress.

'What are you going out like that for?' he asks you one day as you're heading out to walk Satan. 'You look like a tart.'

You look down at your outfit. Okay, maybe the pastry base and strawberry jam topping combo *was* a mistake... But hang on a minute, you can dress how you like! How dare Dean try to tell you what to do?

'I think I look nice,' you tell him defiantly. 'You know I like to show off my assets.'

'To other blokes, you mean!' Dean says angrily.

'I've told you, Babe, you don't need to be jealous,' you say placatingly, wrapping your arms around him. 'You're the only one for me.'

To be honest, you're getting a bit bored by Dean's jealous moods. Lately he's become so paranoid that you're interested in other guys. You've told him 20 times that you were only looking for your keys in that minicab driver's lap. And that blond guy at the pub was giving you mouth-to-mouth after you'd choked on a dry-roasted peanut. But he won't listen.

What can you do to convince him he's the only one?

'How about we get matching tattoos?' you ask, gazing deep into his eyes.

Dean's face brightens a little. 'Yeah, that's a great idea!' he says. 'I've still got a bit of room left on my left arm, under Cathy, Tara, Tina, Kelly, Louise, Courtney and Emma.'

But it seems that even having 'Dean eats here for free' and a big arrow tattooed just above your bikini line isn't enough to placate him. A few days later he blows his top again, this time about your plans to enter the *Search for a Star* competition at the new gastropub that's just opened, The Overpriced Cheese. You're sure you're in with a great chance of winning with your sexed-up version of 'Ave Maria'.

'I don't want you parading up and down on stage being ogled by all those men!' he rages. 'Your body should be for my eyes only.'

'Dean, I just know I was meant to be famous, and this could be my big break,' you tell him. 'Why won't you support my dreams?'

But his eyes are cold as he looks at you. 'If you go in for this competition, we're through.'

'You can't mean that!'

'I do! I mean every single word! When you get back, don't expect me to be here.'

Your heart feels like it's breaking. 'Dean,' you plead, 'don't make me choose!'

Dean has put you in an impossible position. It's like that impossible position he put you in when he gave it to you doggy style over his mum's coffee table and you ended up with your head wedged underneath the sofa. But this is even worse: you risk losing Dean, not just your dignity. What are you going to do?

If you want to save your relationship and stick with Dean, go to 14 on page 61

If you want to enter *Search for a Star*, go to 30 on page 134

2

You're going to be okay, Shampayne, you tell yourself. What is it Nana Rose always says? If life gives you lemons, throw them back in its face and tell it it'd better make sure you get you something useful like an iPad next time, or you'll break its legs.

And at least you've got Swimmy; he's always there for you. You scoop him out of the water and hold him close. His little body throbs and pulses, and his tail thrashes wildly. People dismiss fish as dumb creatures, but they have an innate understanding of human pain. Just look at Swimmy now – it's almost like he's suffering, too.

'Oh Swimmy,' you sigh, 'you're my only friend. If only we could swim away together...'

And that's when you have your most brilliant idea yet. Better than that idea you had about moving your hand away when you accidentally put it over a naked candle flame. You should do a TV show about fish! Yes, that's a fantastic idea! Fish are your passion, after all, and you've read two Ladybird books about them. You're practically David Attenborough.

You call Crispin. 'I've had an idea,' you tell him.

'Really?' Crispin sounds amazed. 'What is it?'

'I want to do a nature programme all about under the sea. It could be on the Discovery Channel or something.'

'Well...' Crispin sounds thoughtful, 'I suppose Kate Humble and Michaela Strachan *are* getting on a bit. You know, maybe you're just what the nature sector needs – a bit of sexing-up, if you know what I mean.'

It's true, nature programmes haven't been all that sexy to date. When the animals make love, there's no nice music or soft lighting or anything. You could work to change all that.

'First things first, I'll have to arrange for you to do a pilot,' Crispin tells you.

'That's okay, I don't need your help with that,' you tell him. 'I know which bars the pilots hang out in.'

'That's not what I mean, Shampayne,' says Crispin, sounding somewhat exasperated. 'A pilot means a one-off episode. To see whether the idea works or not.'

You're sure it will – there's nothing out there quite like it right now. All the other fish programmes you've seen have been totally butch – there's *Robson Dobson's Big Bastard Fish*; *Extreme Fish Wrestling with Steve Maverick*... Your programme's going to be more feminine. You'll offer beauty tips as well as fish information.

'What do you think it should be called?' you muse. 'How about *Shampayne's Deep*?'

Crispin makes a little snorting noise. 'Let's try *Skinny Dipping with Shampayne*.'

Yes, you like it! You've got a great feeling about this.

Ooops, you forgot you were still holding Swimmy! Bless him, he's fallen asleep. You pop him back gently in the water and watch him float. You'll let him have a snooze and wake him later when it's time for his tea.

'They say fish don't really sleep,' you say, gazing into the camera lens, 'but my goldfish Swimmy has been asleep for four weeks now. It just goes to show, there's lots we still don't know about the mysterious world of fish.'

You turn and dive, in a graceful arc, into the sparkling Caribbean waters. Seconds later, you come up for air, the water glistening on your bronzed, naked limbs.

'Look at this little guy here,' you say, pointing down towards a tiny, minnow-like fish that's darting around your legs. 'It's red with black bits on. And this one over here's stripey. Just look at the world around you,' you continue to camera, 'right here on the ocean floor. Such wonderful things surround you, what more is you lookin' for? Under the sea, under the sea...' You're not sure where you're going with this, so you flip over and float on your back in silence for a couple of minutes. Your breasts block out the sun.

After your intro, there's an aerial shot of a coral reef, and a two-minute sequence of you floating on a Lilo wearing only your bikini bottoms. Then there's half an hour of you swimming naked through a shoal of angelfish.

The pilot goes out on Dad TV at 8pm, and guess what? The public love it! Your viewing figures are through the roof!

Of course, there are one or two haters. 'Shampayne Sullivan brings a whole new meaning to plumbing the depths,' gripes TV critic A A Gills.

Wannabe

Dr Heather Guppy, Professor of Fish Studies at Oxford University, moans about you in *The Serious Paper*. 'The woman doesn't know the first thing about fish!' she carps. 'People are only watching her show because she looks good in swimwear.'

But you were expecting some people to be well jel of your new career. You're not going to let them bring you down.

You've landed your dream job, and everything in your life's going brilliantly. Yes, you've finally found your porpoise in life – he's called Flopper, and you got him dirt cheap off eBay because his tail's missing, and he can only swim in circles. He can keep Swimmy company – if only Swimmy would wake up. Perhaps you should take him to the vet? You'd better give him a shower first, though; he's starting to whiff a bit. And you don't want the vet to think you're a neglectful owner, especially now you're a TV nature expert. Yes, once Swimmy is back to full health, you'll have everything you've ever wanted. And why not? You deserve it. You're Shampayne Sullivan!

YOUR CELEBRITY ADVENTURE IS OVER

3

Well, it had to happen sometime. You've had the fame and adulation, now it's time for the backlash. *The Serious Paper* has published an exposé of you in its Saturday magazine.

'Shampayne Sullivan was a tart and a slag and everyone hated her. She used to show off, and flash her bra and knickers at the boys in lessons,' Sandra Bryce, Countryshire Academy's Deputy Head recalls. Maths teacher Richard Arnold is quick to agree with Mrs Bryce's assessment. 'Everyone bitched about her, and threw darts at a picture of her stuck up on the wall. I'm not sure how the pupils felt, but that was definitely how it was in the staffroom.'

Your ex-boyfriends have all come out of the woodwork to add their two cents.

'Shampayne was sex mad,' Dean's reported as saying. 'She'd do anything – and I mean *anything* – in bed. I've never met a girl with a filthier mind. She's cold-hearted, ambitious, and she'll tread on anyone to get what she wants,'

Bless him. At least *he's* not bad-mouthing you.

Still, a backlash always hurts, even if, realistically, you knew it would happen at some point. The public don't like success. And you've achieved more in your 20 years than most people have in a whole lifetime.

The Internet is awash with rumours about you. A fake Twitter profile is set up in your name, in which 'you' bitch about people and witter on inanely about clothes and make-up and generally spout drivel. Wait a minute, that's your real account. Well, apparently there's another, not-real one out there which makes you sound not very nice.

'It always works like that,' sighs Nana Rose. 'The public build you up, and then knock you back down. You're just going to have to tough it out. I can't have *everyone* kneecapped.'

But the worst is still to come. Somehow the press have tracked down your mum in Bali.

'SHAM'S MUM'S DOING BIRD!' screams *The Bun*.

What? They've got that all wrong. Mum may be many things, but she's not a lesbian. She'd *never* do a bird.

Your Twitter followers begin deserting you in droves. Trolls troll you, and Swimmy and Nana Rose, too, which hurts a lot. But all those worries about your declining popularity soon fade to nothing when you face the scariest event of your life. One evening at home, as you're giving yourself a pedicure, you notice a lump.

OMG! You've got a bloody verruca!

Your first reaction is one of sheer terror. Why you? Why now? It's so unfair, you hardly ever go swimming. Nana Rose goes every week and she's never had a verruca in her life!

My God, what if it spreads? You could end up with four, maybe five verrucas on each foot. That happened to someone you knew in primary school. If it gets that bad, you won't be able to wear stilettos or nice sandals this summer.

You fling yourself onto the bed and weep bitter tears. Who'll want you now you're not physically perfect any more? God, you're so alone. Only Swimmy understands how you feel; he nudges against the side of the tank and does a sympathy poo.

Unexpectedly, though, there's an upside to the whole horrible experience.

'SHAM'S PAIN!' reads the *Daily Maul* headline, above a picture of you leaning on Nana Rose's arm, hobbling your way into the doctor's surgery.

'Brave Shampayne Sullivan is being treated for a foot infection at the Cauldwell Clinic in Northwest London,' the story continues. 'Despite being in great discomfort, the former Chix singer has vowed to keep up her punishing schedule of charity work and personal appearances at nightclubs and shopping centres.

'"I want to thank everyone for their support at this difficult time," she commented last night. "Please bear with me if I'm not photographed for a while, or you don't see me wearing heels. I'm going to be concentrating on spending time with my family and pets."'

'"She is still a beautiful girl," "a friend" is quoted as saying, "even though you might think, 'Eurrrgh!' when you think about her feet. No one's going to want to suck her toes any more. But the doctors are doing everything they can. She's a fighter, and she'll come through this."'

Messages of support come flooding in. 'Hang in there, Shampayne, we're all thinking of you,' tweets one fan. 'We love you, Shammi, you're an inspiration,' posts another.

Wannabe

Taylor Swift, Tinie Tempah, Ed Sheeran and Katy Perry don't actually post anything, but you're pretty sure they're thinking of you, too.

And you know what? Having a verruca has made you a better person. As you hobble around in your UGG boots, even though you'd rather be in wedges, you know how it must feel to be disabled, or disfigured in some way. Not smelly or incontinent or unsightly or anything. Just prettily disabled, like a supermodel with a headache.

Slowly, you start responding to treatment. The freezing gel hurts like hell, but the verruca seems to be losing the battle.

'Keep fighting, Shampayne!' Nana Rose urges, as she clutches your hand.

'You can beat this!' your podiatrist assures you.

Right now, you're taking it one day at a time. But if things go your way – and they usually do – you'll be back. You'll slip into your Manolo Blahnik slingbacks again some day. Once more you'll be photographed in 5-inch Jimmy Choo stilettos. It's going to take more than a verruca to keep Shampayne Sullivan down...

YOUR CELEBRITY ADVENTURE IS OVER

4

You marry Dean.
YOUR CELEBRITY ADVENTURE IS OVER

What did you do *that* for? Quick, go back and choose the other option!

5

You can't believe it's taken you so many years to realise you're a lipstick lesbian! If only you'd known that kissing another girl in public would lead to such a media frenzy, you'd have come out years ago.

You're so grateful to Coco, your new girlfriend, for showing you just how rewarding faux lesbianism can be. She's a lingerie model, and she's exotic, dangerous, sexy and super-cool. You look amazing together. When you're apart, you think of nothing else but her. You just want to be pictured with her all the time.

Within days of meeting her, you'd moved into her Central-London bolthole. It's a honeymoon period. You spend your first official evening as girlfriend and girlfriend finding out all about each other. It turns out her favourite singer is Bruno Mars and her fave colour is purple. She loves rabbits. If she could have one superpower it would be invisibility, and the food she likes best is spaghetti.

Now you feel you know her inside and out. This is the most intimate relationship you've ever had. Coco is introducing you to all sorts of new things you've never encountered before: modern art, some stuff called quinoa that tastes like potting soil, and new types of music. She's really into this Russian heavy metal band called Pussy Riot. 'They got put in prison for this,' she says angrily, as you watch a video of theirs set in a church. It seems a bit unfair; they're not exactly Girls Aloud but you didn't think they sounded *that* bad.

At first, Coco seems like the perfect girlfriend. But pretty soon you begin to suspect that she might actually be a *real* lesbian, not just a pretendy one. She wants to do more, sexually, than just snog you when there's paparazzi around. And she's given up shaving her armpits, and is encouraging you to do the same. 'You don't need to be a slave to patriarchy, Shampayne,' she tells you.

'You should come along to my women's group this Thursday,' she says one night, as you're posting up a few sexy gelfies (girl-on-girl selfies – keep up!). 'We're going to be discussing "*The Female Eunuch* and Its Relevance 40 Years On".'

You've absolutely no idea what she's talking about. She might as well be speaking Spanish.

'Come on, it'll be fun!' Coco enthuses, noticing your blank expression. 'Lesley's going to bring borscht.'

You thought Borscht might be Lesley's new puppy. Which explains how you've ended up here, in a draughty church hall at 9pm on a cold, wet Thursday, eating vegetable soup with a bunch of fatties.

'We have a guest of honour here tonight,' announces Marion, Coco's frumpy-looking friend. 'Welcome, Shampayne Sullivan!'

Wannabe

There's a scattering of applause. 'I'm sure we're all dying to hear what Shampayne has to say about the F-word.'

Coco nudges you in the ribs. 'Go on,' she urges. 'Tell them.'

'Um, well, hi there,' you begin. There's a scary-looking emo girl in black sitting just opposite you; she looks like she needs a good wash. Then a good exfoliation. Then toning, pore-stripping, moisturising and fake tanning. In fact, most of these women look like they need urgent cosmetic attention.

'I try not to use the F-word too much,' you explain, 'because I think swearing's a bad habit to get into.'

'Told you she was hilarious, didn't I?' Coco grins.

'Can you tell us what feminism means to you?' the emo girl asks. 'Is it about using men and casting them aside?'

'It's great that you've done that!' pipes up a chubby-faced teenager in a red hoodie. 'You don't take any crap from guys.'

A tough-looking older woman in a leather jacket nods enthusiastically. 'We love that you've just gone out there and taken what you want. You haven't let anything get in your way.'

'Well, I think I *deserve* success,' you say, shrugging your shoulders. 'I *am* special, and gorgeous, and talented.'

Marion beams. 'That's such a great message to give young girls,' she trills. 'You're inspiring them to love themselves, to believe they're amazing.'

Coco squeezes your hand. 'They think you're awesome!' she whispers. 'You should be on TV!'

Wow, you're really enjoying this! All this time you thought you were just a cold-hearted, selfish bitch, but you've actually been a role model all along. Who knew?

Maybe feminism could be a new direction for you? You could maybe let a couple of hairs grow back on your foo-foo and see where it takes you. Whatever you decide, depilation-wise, it's clear there's lots more in store for Shampayne Sullivan. But for now...

YOUR CELEBRITY ADVENTURE IS OVER

6

That's it – your marriage is over. It lasted just 11 months and four days. You throw yourself onto your bed and try to weep bitter tears, but none come. To be honest, you don't really feel anything, but you're probably just numb with grief.

Why didn't things work out? Are you destined to be alone? The only bonus is that the constant media coverage of your breakup has raised your profile to its highest level yet.

Nana Rose and Satan come to stay. It's at times like these that you need your family close. Also, you spent quite a lot doing up that kennel for Reece and you don't want to see it go to waste; Satan loves it.

'Stop moping around, you silly tart,' Nana Rose admonishes you. 'You'll never get famous if you just sit around wallowing.'

She's right, of course. You're still young, gorgeous and D-list-famous. Which means you still get to speak about yourself in the third person. What's next for Shampayne Sullivan?

Wannabe

'I think I'm going to do something to do with fashion,' you tell Nana Rose.

'Yeah, why not? It's a great idea.' Nana Rose is nodding. 'It can't be that hard if Posh Spice has done it.'

The girls lined up before you all look so young and innocent, just as you once were. Well, you were young, at least. Turning them into topless models is a big responsibility, and it's not going to be easy. There's so much more to it than taking off your bra. No, really.

'I see before me 12 beautiful girls, each with an impressive rack,' you read from the autocue. 'But only one of them can be crowned The UK's Top Topless Model.' You frown and look fierce. 'There are no second prizes in this competition,' you say sternly. 'You need to want this, you need to fight.'

The contestants eye each other nervously.

'I'm here to teach you everything I know,' you continue, 'from the poses to the make-up and the haircare. I'm always here for you, girls. I want to support you on your journey...' Your eyes are starting to brim over with tears now. 'Think of me as your best, most gorgeous friend.'

One of the contestants – a pretty redhead – gives a little choking sob.

'Can we call you, if we're worried about something?' asks a statuesque girl with black ringlets.

'If it's going to be filmed, then yes, of course.'

'Even if it's the middle of the night?' asks the redhead.

'I'm Shampayne Sullivan, not Mother Fucking Teresa!' you snap. Honestly, these girls are all me, me, me!

The redhead looks suitably cowed.

'Now, it's time for your first challenge,' you announce. 'Being a topless model is hard work, and this challenge reflects that. You must bring more to the picture than your boobs, you have to bring personality. You have to be able to convey an emotion, a feeling, an essence. This week is our food challenge. Shannon...'

The girl with black ringlets steps forward.

'You are going to be photographed in just your knickers but I want you to convey the spirit of the aubergine.'

Shannon looks puzzled. 'How...?'

You glare at her. 'If you answer back, clients aren't going to want to book you again,' you warn.

'Eliza...' A snub-nosed, bouncy blonde steps forward. 'Your topless shot needs to represent the essence of Cheddar cheese.'

One by one you dish out the challenges to the girls. They're a mixed bunch, but one or two of them are particularly gorgeous and have something really special. You make a mental note to send them home in the first elimination rounds.

You're loving every second of the show. Over the next few weeks you help put the girls through their paces on lingerie shoots and teach them how to look sultry and alluring even when they're feeling ill, or they're oxygen-deprived, submerged in a tank full of sharks or set on fire.

Shannon soons breaks down under the pressure. 'I get really bad PMT,' she sobs. 'I can't look sexy and alluring when I want to kill somebody!'

'There's no PMT in Topless Model!' you bark at her.

'That's not true, actually,' points out Eliza, who turns out to have a degree in semantics. 'There's a p and a t in topless, and an m in...'

You shoot her a withering look. She's going home next.

'Look, Shannon,' you explain, 'you just have to rise above it. Pout, and squoobz.'

That's your catchphrase. Tyra Banks has 'smize' – to 'smile with the eyes'. You have squoobz, to 'squeeze the boobs' together.

The show is a ratings hit; finally the public seem to have warmed to you. The whole *The UK's Top Topless Model* experience has been truly rewarding. It's wonderful to be a guru, to be someone these girls look up to. They want to be just like you. And it's a great feeling, passing on your knowledge to the next generation. It makes you wonder whether your true vocation might not lie outside glamour modelling, in teaching. Could you go back to the classroom, and retrain?

If you want to go into teaching, go to 23 on page 103
If you want to take your TV career to the next level, go to 37 on page 157

7

You can hardly believe it! Your sex tape – the one you made with Kyle, the second love of your life so far, of your most private, intimate, slutty moments – is all over the Internet!

'Sham 69' is the leading search term on Google in the UK right now. You're trending everywhere – you're all over Twitter, and your video is the number-one download not only in Britain, but South Africa and Australia as well. OMG! Who could have done this? Who has betrayed your trust like this?

Oh, that's right, it was you.

You *bastard*!

You throw yourself face-down on the bed and shed bitter tears. This is the hardest lesson in life you've ever had. You're a deceitful, backstabbing liar! All this time, you thought you genuinely cared about yourself, but behind your own back, you were plotting how you could make a quick buck out of yourself, and increase your international profile.

Wannabe

Your mascara makes ugly stains on the bedspread. How can you ever trust yourself again? That's the last time you put your faith in yourself, the last time you make a sex tape where you get to retain all rights to the footage. Never again!

You check your phone messages. There are four from Kyle, who's in London having a hair transplant; you delete them at once. There are tons more from journos at the *Daily Maul* and *The Bun*, several from radio and TV companies, and a final one from Crispin Gay, top PR agent and celebrity spin doctor.

You listen to his voicemail.

'This could be the best thing that's ever happened to you, Shampayne,' Crispin says confidently, his voice like silk. 'Come down to London and see me. We'll work out a media plan for you.'

Could Crispin be right? Might allowing every single person in the world who has access to the Internet a glimpse of your minnie have been a wise move after all? Could the insatiable public appetite for filth actually work in your favour?

Yes, probably.

'Shampayne,' you tell yourself, 'you've got to be strong.' So what if around an estimated 7.2 million people and rising, according to Google stats, have seen everything that God gave you? Well, apart from your bottomhole – you made sure that close-up was edited out. Actually, the movie is pretty tasteful: the lighting is flattering, the camera angles are good, and you've got Kenny G playing in the background. Not the actual guy, obviously, just a CD.

Hell, if anything, you should be proud! Hold your head high, Shampayne. You've nothing to be ashamed of.

You get up from the bed and dry your eyes. You're going to have to face the world some time, so it might as well be now. Just brazen it out.

Wannabe

First off, though, you've got to decide what to wear. You're thinking, 'Nigella Lawson Goes to Court', but see-through. Let's see... You rifle through your wardrobe and pick out a sheer black blouse and lacy mini. Knickers or no knickers? Knickers, you decide – just in case there's a breeze. Now for the face... Just a hint of blusher, and some clear lip balm, to keep things natural. Followed by foundation, concealer, powder, bronzer, fake eyelashes, purple glitter eye shadow, lipliner, lipstick and three top coats of lip gloss.

There's a burst of light as you open your front door, as 100 camera flashes go off at once. You shield your eyes with a perfectly manicured hand.

'Shampayne!' a paparazzo yells. 'Over here!'

'This way, darlin'!' shouts another voice. 'Give us a smile!'

God, this is awful! Why are they hounding you? All you wanted was to live quietly in the media spotlight with your attention-seeking ex-pop star boyfriend.

Tears spring to your eyes, and the flashbulbs pop again. Can't they see you're suffering? These heels are bloody killing you. The sooner you get to London the better.

Bless Nana Rose, she's arranged for an old friend from East London, Jimmy 'Crazyman' Crane, to drive you down there, and he's waiting patiently at the end of the drive. Most of Nana's childhood pals have funny nicknames, like 'Stabber' Harris and Joey 'Wife Murderer' Finn. They sound scary but they're a lovely bunch, always joking about people they've 'buried in Epping Forest', which you think is Cockney Rhyming Slang for something, you're just not sure what.

Jimmy opens the car door for you and you clamber in. He says something in a low voice to the crowd of photographers –

you can't hear what, exactly – and they scatter like a flock of starlings. One of them even drops his camera as he scrambles towards his car. Maybe Jimmy mentioned the fact that the café down the road is doing a 'Buy one, get one free' offer on breakfasts all this week?

The journey into London doesn't take long, and you have just enough time to put the finishing touches to your hair and make-up. You want Crispin Gay to see you at your absolute best. The man's a legend in showbusiness circles. He's handled the sex-tape and kiss-and-tell scandals of most of the UK's bit-part actresses and former reality TV stars.

And he's a billionaire businessman to boot.

He doesn't disappoint in the flesh, either.

'Shampayne! I'm delighted you came.' Crispin kisses you on both cheeks and ushers you into his office. He's an imposing guy: 6ft 3in, piercing grey eyes, wavy, dark-copper hair. He reminds you of someone, but you can't think who.

Crispin stands behind his desk, hands folded behind his back, and gazes at you in silence for a moment. His sparkling grey eyes look amused, as if they're assessing you, peeling back the layers to the soft, yielding parts beneath.

'Thanks for seeing me,' you mumble, blushing fiercely under four layers of MAC Studio Fix Foundation. Why do you suddenly feel embarrassed? You never feel embarrassed – after all you had your shame glands removed when you were seven. This is weird...

'Shampayne,' Crispin murmurs, his lips quirking up into a smile, 'let me tell you how I operate. If you sign a contract with me, I will be your svengali. I will control every aspect of your career. You won't be able to visit a nightclub or restaurant, be seen at a summer festival or on holiday, or attend the opening of a new flagship handbag store without my permission. I will have the final say on what you wear, eat and drink.'

'Do I have to ask you whenever I need the loo?' you ask tentatively.

Crispin wrinkles his perfect nose. 'Er, no. I don't think that will be necessary.'

Your stomach is fluttering with excitement. Wow, you've got your own svengali! You've always wanted one of those since you were a kid! While your classmates were pestering their parents for Barbies or kittens, you always longed for a super-controlling manager who'd micromanage your life down to the ittiest, bittiest detail, to the point of smothering you. This is *bound* to end well.

And it's not long before Crispin gives you your first assignment.

'I want you to take a couple of girl friends and go somewhere hot for a few days,' he tells you. 'Dubai, maybe, or the Caribbean.'

'But I don't have any girl friends...'

'Okay, just go on your own then,' Crispin says irritably. 'I'll send a photographer over with you, he'll take care of all the pictures. All you have to do is walk along the beach topless, looking sad. Then be pictured on your hotel balcony, topless, looking sad. Then frolic, sadly and toplessly, in the waves. Got that?'

It sounds simple enough. 'Got it!' you say.

'Good girl,' he replies, smirking.

Oh my! you think in italics. When he smirks like that he's *so freakin' hot!*

'Hey, Crispin,' you say flirtatiously, 'do you want to come to my hotel room later? We could get to know each other better...'

Crispin's grey eyes widen in alarm; his nostrils flare – he looks like a horse about to bolt. *'I'm* the one in charge, Shampayne,' he says shakily. 'You must never forget that.'

Wannabe

He may be a bit of a control freak, but Crispin turns out to be a great svengali. The newspapers snap up shots of you looking sad and topless in various locations around the South of France. You're inundated with offers from lads' mags to pose both in and out of your pants. *Ooh La La!* magazine does a double-page-spread interview with you, about how you're coping since Kyle so cruelly betrayed your trust.

'He's tried to contact me numerous times,' you tell the reporter tearfully, 'but I never, ever want to talk to him again.'

'That's understandable,' she murmurs sympathetically, offering you a tissue. 'He must have hurt you so badly.'

'I *am* hurt,' you sniff. 'Luckily, I have my fish to keep me strong.' Thank God for Swimmy, he's kept you sane through all of this.

'So, what's next for you, Shampayne?' the reporter asks, trying to lift your mood. 'You're a beautiful woman, have you considered acting, or modelling?'

You dab at your eyes with the tissue. 'It's always been my dream to act,' you admit. 'Ever since you mentioned it, in fact.'

Come to think of it, that's not a bad idea at all. Acting is just pretending, right? How hard can it be?

You phone Crispin. 'Can you get me any acting work?' you ask.

There's a 'thwack!' sound at the end of the line, and a muffled cry.

'Can you hear me, Crispin? Is this a bad line?'

'No, no, it's fine...' Crispin sounds slightly out of breath. 'Acting, you say? Do you have any experience?'

'No,' you admit. 'But I'm really, really good at pretending stuff. Like being in love, and enjoying bad sex, and things like that.'

'Well...' Crispin goes quiet for a few moments. 'I do have

a casting-agent friend who's looking for some new faces for *Oakyholes*. I'll have a word with her about you.'

Oakyholes? Wow, that's one of the longest-running soaps on TV! You'd love to be in that!

'Should I do anything to prepare?' you ask eagerly. 'Like, maybe take an acting class or something?'

'Nah, don't bother with that,' Crispin says casually. 'Just wax your bikini line.'

There's a low, muffled moan at the other end of the line. 'Gotta go,' Crispin abruptly announces before hanging up.

You don't expect to hear from Crispin again until he's sorted out the audition but that evening, you find a voicemail message from him on your phone.

'There is something about you that intrigues me,' he says huskily. 'It's your vulnerability, your innocence...'

Oops, he's sent this to the wrong person! But hang on a minute, it IS for you...

'Shampayne, I want to show you my special Red Room of Pain,' the message continues, '*if* you dare. Come to see me at my mansion tomorrow. Laters, Baby.'

Eurgh, it's a bit creepy! And who says 'Laters, Baby' unless they've been beamed in from 1997? But you have to admit part of you is curious. What exactly *is* Crispin's Red Room of Pain?

If you want to give Crispin a wide berth and just audition for *Oakyholes*, go to 39 on page 162

If you want to check out Crispin's Red Room of Pain, go to 9 on page 39

8

The Golden Globes are coming up, and you need to look your absolute best. So it's off to see celebrity facialist Charlotte Tan to find out what new treatments she has to offer. She's the best in her field – always the first to offer the most radical new procedures – and all the A-list actresses beat a path to her door around this time of year.

At Charlotte's Santa Monica salon you've been nibbled by tiny fish, had snake venom and sheep placenta cells injected into your face, been scrubbed down with coffee grounds, bathed in holy water, covered in gold leaf and coated with monkey sperm. You could have sued over that last incident but you didn't – it wasn't Charlotte's fault that her pet macaque worked out how to undo the lock on his cage.

Charlotte looks delighted to see you. 'You've got to try our new Mug Facial,' she says. 'You won't believe the results!'

'A Mug Facial? Is it like that cupping treatment I had?' you ask eagerly. 'I really liked that one, where you and the girls put your tea cups all over me. It was so relaxing...'

Charlotte laughs. 'Oh yes, that was a good one, wasn't it? No, this is one of our new, non-invasive facials. We don't actually need to touch your skin at all.'

'So how does it work?' you ask, intrigued.

'We simply remove money from your bank account with a gentle fleecing motion, to make it feel instantly lighter and less bloated.'

'Wow!' you say. 'It sounds amazing!'

'It is,' Charlotte assures you. 'You're going to love it. Shall I book you in for this week?'

'Ooooh, yes, please!' you cry. 'If I have it done now, do you think I'll see results by Saturday? I want to look as good as I can on the red carpet.'

'Oh, the effects will have definitely kicked in by then,' murmurs Charlotte, logging your appointment into the computer. 'So, we'll do the treatment on Thursday, at 3.20pm.'

'Great,' you say, 'I'll see you then.'

'Oh, you don't need to come in,' Charlotte tells you. 'It's all done remotely.'

What an innovation! The beauty industry certainly knows how to move with the times.

'Don't forget we're running a 2-for-1 offer this week!' Charlotte calls after you as you leave. 'Which means we'll be charging your credit card twice instead of once.'

That's your skin sorted. But what about a dress? Who do you think always looks classy and classic? Cate Blanchett, for sure. Nicole Kidman, Jennifer Aniston... Well, you don't want to look as boring as them. You'd better go on the hunt for something see-through.

You'll need a drastic diet, too. Currently you're 8st 2lb, of which 11lb is your breasts; if you could lose 1lb or 2lb it would make all the difference.

You call into you favourite juice bar for a bee pollen and beetroot smoothie, but on your way out, you collide with a tall, handsome, bearded guy coming the other way.

'I'm so terribly sorry,' he says. 'Oh my, I seem to have made you spill your smoothie. Well, this is just dreadful!'

OMG, it's Eton-educated posh-boy actor Quentin Hythe-Percy! And he's even more gorgeous in the flesh than he was in that film about the World War I donkey sanctuary!

'It's okay,' you say, 'I didn't really need the calories.'

'Do allow me to buy you another one.' He lifts his sunglasses and looks at you properly. 'I say, aren't you Shampayne Sullivan? May I just say, I greatly admire your work?'

You'd blush, if you were actually still capable of feeling embarrassment. But instead you just run your tongue slowly over your lips and undo a couple of buttons on your shirt-dress. You're not going to let this one get away...

At first Quentin seems like the perfect boyfriend. But pretty soon you realise that he's probably the nicest person you've ever met.

He insists on Skyping his mum a few times a week because since his dad died last year, 'she's struggled to cope' or something.

He'd rather go for a meal with you than to a club with groupies and hangers-on because 'those people are fake', and anyway, he'd 'rather be with you'.

He refuses to let his ex-girlfriends Shelley and Abi join you in bed because he 'doesn't need anyone else' but you. Ditto Raoul the handyman, his mates Gareth and Niall, and Niall's mum and dad, who are visiting from Belfast. So it's just the two of you. You can honestly say you've never had a more boring time in bed, except that one time when you were home alone and you tried to read a book.

God, Quentin's nice. He hasn't even looked at another girl, not once, let alone been caught sexting. He's always so considerate, forgiving, tolerant and funny.

You're not sure you can take this shit any more.

The final straw comes when he asks you to fly over to England with him for a few days, at his expense, to meet his family. 'I've told them all about you,' he says, stroking your hair tenderly. 'They think you sound amazing.'

Jesus, you must be the only actress in Hollywood being treated this way! You're going to have to tell Quentin it's never going to work. But not right this minute, because tomorrow he's promised to knock up some built-in shelves for your living room.

'This is never going to work, Quentin,' you murmur the next day, as he's wiring in some spotlights above the top shelf.

'Don't you like it?' he asks, stepping back to admire his handi-work. 'I can make alterations, if you like.'

'It's not the shelving,' you say, sadly. 'It's great. Although maybe you could lower that middle shelf by a few inches?'

Quentin picks up his hammer.

You suppose your chat can wait a little longer...

An hour later, you try again. 'It's not me, it's you,' you tell him gently. 'You're a great guy and everything, but I need someone in my life who's frankly a bit more of a shit.'

Quentin looks pained. 'What you're saying is... I'm too nice?'

You nod. 'I just need... oh, I don't know, maybe more of a creep, or a loser, to complete me. Some low-life who'll happily live off my earnings in my luxury condo, then do the dirty on me with an eighteen-year-old pole dancer called Misti-Lou.'

'Would it help if I sleazed a bit more?' Quentin says. The desperation in his voice is clear. 'I can sleaze... Please, Shampayne, let me sleaze...'

Tears are pooling in your eyes now; you don't deserve this.

'Look!' he says, pulling his phone from his pocket. 'I'm going to take a picture of my genitals *right now*, and I'm going to send it to... to.... to Nana Rose!'

You smile through your tears. 'Oh Quentin, I can see you're trying but it's too late,' you tell him sadly. 'You should at least have bad-mouthed me to the press by now, or been caught with a couple of underage escort girls.'

His shoulders sag. 'You're right,' he says mournfully. 'I've been an idiot. I can't go round treating women like this – making shelving systems, cooking delicious meals, rescuing puppies... This is Hollywood, for God's sake.'

You stroke his hand gently. 'That's your personal struggle,' you murmur. 'I know you've got issues, but I have faith in you; you'll work on them. Someday, when you're more of an asshole, I know you'll make at least one gullible Hollywood actress briefly happy before you clean out her bank account and force her to pay alimony even though you've never done a single day's work in your lousy life.'

Quentin clasps you to his chest. 'Goodbye, my darling,' he says, his voice cracking with emotion. 'I'll always love you.'

You stare deep into his eyes.

'I'll always love me, too.'

Quentin turns away. 'I guess I'll have to cast someone else now,' he says tearfully.

Wannabe

Come again?

'Sorry, what did you say?'

'Oh, I'm in talks to direct a sequel to *The Donkeys of Mons*,' he says, shrugging. 'It's going to be a musical this time. Benedict Cumberbatch is on board, so's Ralph Fiennes. And I thought you'd be great for the female lead. But I'd find it too hard, working with you, now we've split. Seeing you every day would kill me.'

Your heart leaps. This could be your big chance! Suddenly Quentin seems irresistibly attractive. Should you take him back, even though he's treated you so nicely? Or should you keep your self-respect, and move on?

If you want to take Quentin back, go to 53 on page 218

If you want to move on, go to 19 on page 83

9

Oh my! Crispin's Red Room of Pain is not what you thought it was going to be!

You'd imagined a kinky sex dungeon, maybe, with a rack, and some shackles and a few riding crops hanging up on the wall. But *this*? This is just an ordinary sitting room, with a chintzy couch, a plasma TV, a coffee table scattered with issues of *Fish Fancier* and some cat posters on the walls.

You're confused. 'How is this a Red Room of Pain?' you ask, looking directly into Crispin's steely grey eyes. They're giving nothing away.

'I didn't say Red Room of Pain, I said Red Room of *Payne*,' Crispin retorts. 'As in Sham*payne*.'

'You clearly said, "Pain".'

'Didn't.'

'Did.'

'Did not.'

'Did, too.' This could go on all day.

'Whatever..' you snap. 'So you don't have a sex dungeon?'

'Of course not!' splutters Crispin. 'Sex isn't my bag, Shampayne!' For a brief second he looks lost, like a little boy who can't find his mummy. You want to hold him, to take away the pain. Then his eyes grow cold again.

'I don't make love,' he says firmly, his lips quirking up into an ironic sneer. 'I fuck over my clients.'

Well, that much is true – Crispin's taking 85 per cent of everything you earn.

'So what's with the room?'

Crispin shrugs. 'Each of my clients has a special room at my house, for their personal use. It's useful if you're being hounded by the paparazzi, or you just want to lie low for a while – it's all part of the service.'

You look around. It's clear Crispin has put some thought into this; his ultra-controlling personality is evident in the fine details – he's even decorated a tiny fish tank with sequins for Swimmy.

'So everyone has one?'

'That's right. Next door to this is the Crimson Chamber of Kinkiness, where Ray Davis often stays. And just down the corridor is the Silver Salon of Sin, which belongs to Sinitta.'

'You have to be careful with the names you give these places, Crispin,' you say reprovingly. 'They're a bit misleading. Someone might take them the wrong way.'

Someone like you, to be exact. Truth be told, you're a bit disappointed that Crispin isn't about to lash you to a St Albert's cross, pound your backside with a paddle and ravish you, take you for rides in his helicopter and for meals in the world's most expensive restaurants, tie you to a bed frame and whip your privates with a cat o' nine tails, and fall inexorably in love with you. It would be the perfect end to your story.

Suddenly, Crispin whips out a measuring tape from his pocket. 'Those cushions are misaligned!' he tuts, striding towards the sofa. 'By at least 13cm, I'd say.'

On second thoughts, maybe you should just make your excuses and leave...

'Oh well, I'd best be off,' you say nonchalantly. 'Places to go, people to see...'

You leave Crispin plumping and rearranging the cushions, and head down the corridor towards the marble staircase that leads to the lobby. There's a tall, dark-haired guy coming in the opposite direction; he looks kind of familiar. Wait a second – OMG, it *is* him! It's soul singer Bobbie Dicke! He's an international megastar, known for his respectful, adulatory songs about women, like his worldwide smash hits, 'Shall We Enjoy Some Mutually Consensual Sex Tonight?' and 'You're Not a Bad Girl, or a Good One – I Refuse to Label You'. He must be a client of Crispin's.

Do you dare to introduce yourself, or are you too starstruck?

If you introduce yourself, go to 13 on page 57
If you walk on by, go to 33 on page 146

10

You throw yourself on the bed and shed bitter tears. Why? Why has everything gone so wrong? You were on your way to global notoriety, and now your dreams are in tatters! It's so unfair! You bury your tear-stained face in the satin pillow and howl like a wounded animal.

There's a gentle tapping on your shoulder. 'Madam, the store closes in five minutes,' the sales assistant says tentatively.

You turn your mascara-streaked face towards her. She looks embarrassed, but she should be used to this, you think. You're pretty sure you're not the first person to have a breakdown in the Bedroom Aisle at Ikea.

You guess you'd better be going anyway; this place always has a negative effect on you. You only popped in for some new soup bowls, and now look at you! You gather up your bag and jacket and heave yourself off the bed.

A young couple with a toddler in tow are nudging each

other and whispering; the man's taking pictures of you with his smartphone.

'Yes,' you snap, 'it's me. Shampayne Sullivan. From the Bobbie Dicke video.'

Their toddler's tiny face crumples. 'Mummy!' he wails, 'Scary lady!', and grabs hold of the woman's skirt.

You catch sight of yourself in a wardrobe mirror. God, you look terrible! You haven't washed your extensions for a week. There's eyeliner smudged underneath your bleary eyes; you're pasty and pale. You look like you need a good meal and a sunbed session. And when the smartphone pictures appear on Twitter later that afternoon, it seems the general public agrees.

'Loving Shampayne Sullivan's new style direction #edgy,' tweets someone in Hoxton.

'Some punk-rock shit's going down here,' tweets another hipster. 'Is Shampayne the new Courtney Love?'

Crispin's delighted. 'People are loving the new look, it's really now,' he enthuses. 'Keep on doing what you're doing. We might be able to get you some fashion work.'

It's incredible, really. You flashed a nipple at the Queen and haven't taken a shower in days, and suddenly you're cool. Trendy magazine *Twatscene* publishes an in-depth profile of you, informing hipsters that it's okay to like you non-ironically. And within days, Crispin's fielding requests from urban brands and style bibles for photoshoots and interviews.

Your first booking is a shoot for achingly trendy fashion house Horse/Horse/Hatstand, at a disused public toilet in Bermondsey. The designer is a twenty-one-year-old Central Saint Martins graduate called Kiko, who's so cool that he's evolved beyond speech, and just communicates by making little beeping noises.

Thankfully, he has three or four lackeys to translate for him, otherwise you wouldn't have a bloody clue what to do.

The stylists help you into the first outfit: a giant teapot made of figs, teamed with ripped leggings and biker boots. To be honest, you feel like a bit of an idiot in it, but all that's quickly forgotten when one of the stylists pushes you down a spiral staircase. 'For a more natural pose,' he explains as you land in a heap on the concrete floor, four feet below.

Next, you're naked but for purple fake-fur merkin, and a pair of deely-boppers.

'Um, is this fashion?' you ask tentatively. You've really no idea.

'Beep!' says Kiko, angrily.

After that you just keep quiet. You try not to smile, because every time you do Kiko starts beeping like a malfunctioning fire alarm. But you're starting to get on his wavelength, and understand what he wants: you just have to look vacant and stare into the middle distance, as if your brain's been replaced with pineapple jelly. It's something that comes to you naturally.

'That's it, Shampayne!' one of Kiko's lackeys enthuses, as you curl into a foetal position and start licking the concrete floor. 'You're really interpreting the brand.'

Hey, this cool stuff is actually quite easy! Maybe you've found your niche at last?

'You could become the new Kate Moss!' Crispin enthuses. 'Now all you need to do is get yourself a bunch of seriously wanky mates and go out a lot.'

You have to admit, being the new Mossy would be incredible. But then again, shouldn't you be trying to break into acting? Isn't that what models are supposed to do?

Wannabe

'What do you think, Swimmy?' you ask your aquatic friend. 'Acting or modelling?'

But he's sitting on the fence. Maybe he'd be able to think better if you take him *off* the fence and put him back in his tank?

If you want to be the new Kate Moss, go to 15 on page 67
If you want to try acting, go to 42 on page 172

11

You can't believe it – you're pregnant! How did it happen, you wonder? You and Andy were always so careful. You nearly always did oral, or Andy shagged the random girl you brought home rather than you, so how you've ended up in this state is a bit of a mystery.

God, this is going to *ruin* your figure! Even the yummy mummies at your gym have porridgey tummies and saggy boobs, and those revolting road-map veins on their chests. Well, that's NOT going to happen to you! You're going on a major diet so you have the teensy-weensiest baby of all time – the size of an orange would be about right – which means your stomach will barely stretch at all. And you'll bottle-feed, of course, because everyone knows breastfeeding *destroys* your boobs.

You're feeling a bit less panicky now. Yes, a small baby is definitely best. It'll be cute, like those miniature pigs everyone's buying. Or like a chihuahua. You can pop it in a clutch bag – it'll look adorable!

Wannabe

Maybe this whole pregnancy thing will work to your advantage? After all, all the magazines love a 'meet my new baby' feature. And look at all the interest in Blue Ivy and North West, they're stars in their own right. Yes, this could all work out fine. But first, you've got to share this amazing news with the people in your life who matter.

WTF!Uptheduff!#buninoven, you tweet. It's good to keep your 22,000 followers updated.

You suppose you'd better let Andy know, too. Mad Uncle Freddie was the one who tracked him down; apparently, they took a little jaunt to the country together for a couple of weeks. Andy must've tripped over a stile or something on one of their nature rambles because he's come back with two broken legs and three teeth missing.

You're not sure how Andy's going to feel about becoming a father again. After all, he's only recently had a baby with his last fiancée, and there's the twins he had with the fiancée before that, and the teenage son he had with his first-ever fiancée... You think there might be a couple more kids knocking round somewhere, too. Oh well, in for a penny, in for a pound.

You call Andy's number.

'I thought you ought to know,' you tell him. 'I'm having a baby.'

'I'm pweased for you!' Andy lisps. Those missing teeth will be a bit of a drawback for his TV career. 'Whose is it?'

'It's yours, of course!' you snap. 'Whose did you think it was?'

'But we were awways careful! You onwy give me bwowjobs.'

'Well, I must have swallowed some, obviously.' God, he's thick. He pauses. 'Are you actuawy having it?'

'Yeah, I think so,' you reply. 'It could be the best thing that's ever happened to me.'

He sighs. 'I dunno, I can't seem to keep twack of aw my kids these days.'

'You should get a calendar,' you suggest. 'Some of them have cats on or things like that. Then you can write down all your kids' names and their birthdays and stuff on that.'

'That's a gweat idea!' he says, more cheerily now. 'I hope the kid gets your bwains, Shampayne.'

You're glad you've cleared the air with Andy. It's time to move on; there's so much to buy and so much to do to get ready for the baby. You've decided it will live with Nana Rose for the first few years so you can get on with work. Nana Rose is delighted.

'It'll be so lovely to have something to keep me busy,' she says. 'I've been looking for something to get my teeth into. So has Satan.'

You're feeling sick every morning but that's great, as you always bring up your breakfast. Whenever you feel like eating anything, you just repeat 'Teeny-tiny baby, teeny-tiny baby' under your breath. It's the best diet mantra ever. In fact, you're still just 8 stone a week before the birth.

The delivery isn't so easy, though. Your midwife tries using forceps, and ventouse, but neither works. Now you're getting desperate – you're not sure how much longer you can stand the pain.

'Try diamonds!' you puff, as a new contraction takes hold. Nana Rose hands the midwife your Tiffany bracelet. She dangles it just outside your vagina and, miraculously, a tiny hand comes shooting out.

She's here at last! Sparkles Apricot Rainbow Sullivan. She looks perfect, and you're so relieved that she's attractive. And that your minny didn't turn inside-out, like some mums you hear about.

The midwife wraps Sparkles in a blanket.

Wannabe

'Here's your daughter,' she smiles.

'Hi there, beautiful,' you say, gazing at your reflection in the mirror across the room. How is it that you even look great minutes after giving birth? You're *sooooo* hot!

'Don't you want to hold her?' the midwife asks.

'Nana Rose!' you call out. 'Can you take her for a minute? I need to tweet this.'

Nana Rose bustles over and takes Sparkles in her arms. You get out your iPhone and take a selfie of your tanned legs. There's a little bit of crusty blood at the top of your thighs, but you figure no one will really notice.

'Got rid of the baby bump#readytoparty' you key in.

Right, you've done motherhood. What's next? You should probably get your body back into tip-top shape if you want to be back in your skinny jeans before the fortnight's out. Then again, shouldn't you just take some time out to relax and enjoy your new baby, whatsername?

What's your priority?

If you want to get back into shape, go to 34 on page 148
If you want to become an earth mother, go and live in Brighton or something.

12

You've always dreamed of getting married: a proper white wedding, with a horse-drawn carriage, a beautiful meringue of a dress, and everyone's eyes on you. Why can't you have what every other female C-list celebrity seems to have had – an ill-advised, rushed-into starter marriage lasting anywhere from two months to two years, to a not-very-bright, preferably younger guy, who earns about a twentieth of what you do?

But where are you going to find someone like that?

You throw open your window and look down into the street below. There's a middle-aged woman and two teenagers waiting at the bus stop; an old man shuffles along, pulling a battered shopping trolley, and a youngish-looking guy on a pizza-delivery moped. 'Mmmm, not bad!' you think. He's got everything you look for in a man: two legs, two arms and a head.

'Hey, pizza boy!' you yell.

He looks up. Well, he's obviously not deaf or anything. That's a bonus!

'Do you wanna be my fiancé?'

'And that, in a nutshell, is how I met Reece.'

'What an incredible story!' sighs the *Ooh La La!* reporter. 'It's really romantic. Love at first sight!'

'That's right, it was,' you smile, giving Reece's hand a squeeze. 'I think it was probably korma. We were just meant to be together.'

The reporter glances down at her notebook. 'Reece, what did you think of Shampayne when you first set eyes on her?'

He looks at you questioningly.

'It's okay, Reece. Go ahead, you can speak,' you tell him.

Reece relaxes. 'Well, I was worried first of all that she might topple out the window.'

'I *am* rather top heavy,' you acknowledge.

'And then I thought, "Cor, is that Shampayne Sullivan?" I'd always fancied her; I used to have her poster on my wall in the Young Offenders' Unit.'

'Gosh, what a lovely coincidence!' gushes the reporter. 'So how long after that first meeting was it that you knew she was "The One"?'

'Oh, straight away!' says Reece. 'Because she told me she was. She said we'd be getting married in two weeks.'

'You certainly seem to know what you want, Shampayne.'

'Well,' you simper, 'I couldn't afford to let this one get away.'

'And how does Reece measure up against your previous boyfriends? What does he have that they didn't?'

Oooh, she's thrown you a curve ball! You'll have to think about it for a minute.

'He's blond,' you eventually say. 'All my other boyfriends have had dark hair.'

Good answer. The reporter's nodding.

'And is there anything you'd like to say to those people who might be worried you're rushing into marriage?'

'It does look like we're rushing things a bit, but I know it'll work,' you say confidently. 'Because I'm a Pisces and he's a Libra; so I'm a fish, and he's a set of scales. And what do fish have? Scales!'

The reporter looks puzzled. She's obviously not a deeply spiritual person like you are.

'Okay, one last question: will we be hearing the patter of tiny feet soon?'

Reece perks up at once. 'Are the pixies coming?' he asks excitedly, looking around the room. 'Why didn't anyone tell me the pixies might come?'

My God, he's even thicker than you thought.

You point to the corner of the room. 'Reece,' you say sternly, 'in your basket!'

Reece hangs his head. Dejectedly, he slopes across to the bed you've made for him, out of an old duvet and some towels. He sits down, looking disconsolate. He was *so* looking forward to the pixies.

'Good boy!' you say, beaming. You chuck him a biscuit from the coffee table, which he wolfs down in one gulp. Bless him! He's going to be the perfect starter husband. You'll have him neutered in six weeks.

Your wedding is everything you ever hoped it would be: five spreads in *Ooh La La!*, with a Honeymoon Special to be published the following week, and an Anniversary Issue due next spring if the marriage actually lasts a year. You've dreamt of this pay cheque since you were a little girl. And now here it is at last, in your bank account.

As for the ceremony, it goes off without a hitch. Reece manages to turn up at 3pm on the dot, thanks to the Baby's First Tell the Time talking watch you bought him. You look stunning in your ivory silk brocade basque and matching tanga briefs; there are gasps of 'Oooh!' and 'Oh my Christ!' from the congregation as you make your way down the aisle. You did consider wearing something a bit more demure on your bottom half, but you believe a bride's outfit should highlight her best features. Which in your case are your buttocks.

The one thing that makes you sad is that your mum and dad can't be there to give you away, but you guess they must still be enjoying their Balinese holiday. Still, Nana Rose is there, with a tear in her eye and Satan in her lap.

And, of course, your half of the church is packed out with Z-list celebrities you barely know who want to be in the next issue of *Oooh La La!* It's like a beautiful dream.

Your vows are the most touching part of the ceremony. You've written them for both of you.

'I, Reece, promise to love and obey you, Shampayne. To honour and defer to you, worship and look up to you, as long as you tell me to.'

You gaze up into Reece's eyes. It's like looking into a shallow pool, full of particularly stupid fish.

'I, Shampayne, promise to nurture and direct you, Reece, to guide and control you, so long as I feel like it and media interest demands it.'

'I now declare you woman and husband,' the vicar beams.

Wannabe

Oh wow, that's it! Your first marriage! You can hardly believe this fairy-tale romance has had a happy ending, at least for a little while.

At first Reece seems like the perfect husband, but his IQ soon becomes an issue. You're not prejudiced – you're happy to date thickos, boneheads, idiots, dimwits, halfwits and plonkers – but Reece is something else entirely.

'It's exhausting having to translate everything for him, from English into Reece-ese. He thinks cheese comes from cheeseplants, butter comes from butterflies, and milk comes from cows.

Really, you should dump Reece and move on. The only problem is, your reality show, *Shampayne and Reece: Can You Believe These Two Are For F***ing Real?*, is a ratings hit. And Reece is popular with the public. He's getting his own fanmail now, and there are Facebook sites dedicated to his words of non-wisdom. If you don't do something to destroy his confidence – and quickly – before you know it, he'll have his own brand of aftershave.

'I've written a song,' he tells you one lunchtime, as you're dishing up his Winalot. 'It's called "Inpainia".'

You have to admit, you're a little intrigued. Maybe Reece has been hiding his light under a bushel? He may not be the brightest of sparks, but musical talent has nothing to do with intellect – just look at Justin Bieber.

'Come on, then,' you say impatiently. 'Let's hear it!'

Reece looks suddenly shy. 'Oh, I dunno, Shampayne. I'm still working on the lyrics…'

'Just bloody get on with it then!'

'Okay, then.' Reece gives you one of his goofy grins. 'Wait a minute, I'll just get my keyboard.'

Wannabe

Reece goes over to his toy box and rummages around. He pulls out his Fisher Price Singalong Xylophone, and hammers out a three-note tune.

'People, the world is a crazy place,' he sings, before continuing:
I sometimes wonder, what's going to happen next?
Honestly, some mad shit is going down
Like, it rains all summer, and the winters are really mild.
If we get our seasons all mixed up like that
No one's going to know what to wear.
Ooh, ooh, I'm in pain-ia! Ooh, ooh, I'm in pain-ia!
I was in the supermarket queue the other day...'

You know what, this actually isn't bad! He's certainly better than that Peter Andre. You're going to have to nip this in the bud...

'...and the woman behind the till told me
They're no longer doing buy one, get one free on Mini Cheddars...'

Reece is still singing.

'I mean, that's just mad, isn't it?
That was a really good offer and...'

'Okay!' you bark. 'I've heard enough.'

'What do you think?' Reece asks anxiously.

'It's shit,' you say. 'You're a talentless, pointless waste of space and I don't know what I'm doing being married to you.'

Reece hangs his head. 'Sorry, Shampayne,' he mumbles. 'I just thought maybe I could...' He tails off.

'I didn't marry you so you could have ideas of your own,' you tell him. 'Especially if they're crap ones like that.'

Reece gets down on his knees and crawls towards his dog basket, his genitals hanging between his legs.

It seems cruel, but the thing is with starter husbands, you have to put them in their place, let them know their place in the pack. You've read all the manuals.

Reece, you conclude, is still good for one thing at least: sperm. You think it's high time you had a baby, and he'd be as good a donor as any. Well, that's not strictly true – your baby's IQ will probably be lower than a peanut's. But it'll be good-looking, and that's what matters.

Divorce, or baby? Divorce, or baby? You can't decide...

If you want to get rid of Reece, go to 6 on page 22
If you want to have Reece's baby, go to 27 on page 119

13

Introducing yourself to Bobbie Dicke is the best thing you ever did. It turns out he's looking for models to star in the video for his new song, 'There's a Casserole in the Oven, Darling', and you fit the bill exactly.

'I'll be in the kitchen, cooking,' Bobbie explains, 'and there'll be you, and some other models, dancing around in your business suits, like you've just come back from a boardroom meeting.'

'I've got a better idea!' you say excitedly. 'How about we prance about in the nude while you sing?'

Bobbie frowns. 'Would I be in the nude, too?'

'No, you can wear a suit.'

He doesn't look convinced.

'It'll be fun!' you enthuse. 'Bring your friends. They can be fully clothed too.'

'I don't know, Shampayne. It all sounds a bit misogynistic.'

'A bit what?'

'A bit demeaning.'

'A bit what?'

'A bit... Look, I'm just not comfortable with the idea.'

Honestly, you're amazed Bobbie Dicke's managed to have any hit records at all, given that he doesn't feature any scantily-clad women in his videos. Think what he could achieve if he did!

The video turns out to be Bobbie's dullest yet. No one flashes so much as an ankle. Nevertheless, the song's got a catchy chorus – 'Ain't no gender, that's better with a blender' – and it goes straight in at number one.

'And here's the best news of all: Bobbie's been asked to appear at the Royal Variety Performance, and you'll be on stage with him! Her Majesty the Queen will be in the audience, and William, Harry and Kate Middleclass, too. This is incredible! Who'd have thought that you, Shampayne Sullivan, would one day be performing for the heads of the royal family? It's especially gob-smacking given that you have absolutely no discernible talents. Well, it just goes to prove Nana Rose's old saying is true: if you want something badly enough and you're gorgeous with big knockers, you can usually get it.

Bobbie will be performing his biggest hit to date, 'I'm Attracted To Your Strong Personality'. As it's a family-friendly show, he's made sure your routine isn't raunchy or suggestive, and you and the other backing dancers will be wearing floor-length skirts and baggy sweatshirts.

Nevertheless, you're determined to get noticed. You'll be standing centre-stage for most of the song, just behind Bobbie, and you'll give the routine everything you've got. You're going to blow Prince William's socks off; you'll settle for just blowing Prince Harry.

Wannabe

What would be tasteful and yet showstopping? It's at times like these that you ask yourself: what would Miley Cyrus do? You need to do that, and then some.

That's it, you should twerk, with your tongue hanging out, and maybe one nipple peeking out as well! Yes, that's a great idea! You should probably run it past Bobbie, or the other girls, but what the hell... It can be a surprise on the night.

And it IS a surprise. Prince William almost jumps out of his skin when you grind up against him as he attempts to congratulate you on your performance. The Queen barely blinks when your other nipple pops out, too, but then again social *faux pas* don't ever faze her, she's married to Prince Philip.

Your moves certainly get you noticed in the press. 'SHAMPAYNE'S A TWERKING DISGRACE!' screams *The Bun*. 'WE ARE NOT AMUSED!' roars the *Daily Maul*. It turns out that rubbing one's genitalia against royal nether regions is 'unacceptable' and 'bordering on treason'. Honestly, you can't understand what all the fuss is about. It's not like you used a giant foam finger to poke Kate Middleclass in the boobs or anything. Oh, wait a minute, you did...

Bobbie is fuming. 'This is really bad publicity for me,' he storms. 'I'm a role model for kids, for God's sake! If nine-year-old girls stop buying my records, I'm done for.'

'Oh, come on,' you say, rolling your eyes and poking out your tongue. 'I was just expressing myself, and my sexuality.'

'What's this thing with your tongue hanging out?' Bobbie asks irritably. 'I mean, what are you trying to say?'

'That I'm eating an invisible ice cream?' It's worth a try.

'It's no good, Shampayne, you've damaged my brand,' Bobbie sighs. 'You won't be able to appear on my world tour.'

Wannabe

What? You're Shampayne Sullivan! The live show wouldn't be anything without your input. He can't sack you!

But it turns out he can. Bobbie has you replaced with a lifesize poster of yourself, and no one seems to notice the difference.

You're devastated. One minute you were a backing dancer for one of the world's leading R&B stars, now you're jobless, broke, and alone.

You've hit rock bottom. What are you going to do now?

If you give in to misery and despair, go to 10 on page 42

If you believe the only way is up, go to 2 on page 9

14

It's no good, you can't risk losing Dean. He means the world to you. You'll just have to put your dreams on hold, at least for now. Someday, you'll get your big break, you're sure of that. After all, everyone knows if you want something badly enough, it'll happen. Except if you want a pet unicorn. Or you want to be a brain surgeon and you're thick as a pile of bricks.

'Cheer up, love,' says Nana Rose, as you mope around at home in your off-the-shoulder lace midi-dress, diamanté wedges and full make-up. 'There'll be other opportunities.'

'I know, but I'm just so sick of waiting!' you complain.

Nana Rose claps her hands. 'What you need is a good night out to cheer yourself up,' she says. 'Come on, get your gladrags on; you and me are going out on the razz.'

Four hours later, you and Nana Rose are ready to hit the town. Or at least you would be if there was a town within 30 miles. You'll have to settle for hitting the village instead.

Wannabe

Nana has an impressive figure for a sixty-five-year-old, and looks stunning in a leopard-print mini and a matching bustier, which enhances her dowager's hump. You've kept things casual, in hotpants, heels and a boob tube, fake eyelashes and four layers of fake tan. After all, it's only the local pub, the Bull & Banker.

But it turns out the pub is *the* place to be tonight. There's going to be a band playing, and everyone who's anyone in the village has turned out.

'Ladies and gentlemen!' the landlord calls above the din. 'Singing some new material from his yet-to-be-released solo album, we are very pleased to present... the bald one out of Boylove!'

OMG! Can it really be true?

Boylove were *the* biggest boyband in the UK back in the 1990s. Some of your earliest childhood memories are of your dad singing along to their hits, 'Please, Please Be Mine' and 'Marry Me, Angel', or their last, international number-one smash, 'Things Don't Feel the Same (Down There, Since You Had Our Baby)'. And Keiran O'Reilly, the lead singer, was your first-ever childhood crush; you used to kiss his poster every night before you went to bed.

Admittedly, you don't really remember the bald one, but he's going to be here, any second, up there in front of you! Someone who used to be sort-of famous! If only that short, fat roadie fiddling with the microphone would get off the stage...

'Hi there, thanks for coming!' says the short, fat roadie in a lilting Irish voice.

Oh.

Time hasn't been kind to the bald one out of Boylove. He's now also the paunchy, wrinkled, badly dressed one as well.

Still, never mind. There'll still be a bit of stardust clinging to him, you figure. And maybe, if you get close enough, a bit of it will rub off on you too.

It soon becomes clear that the bald one out of Boylove would like to rub something off on you, though not necessarily stardust.

You get up to dance – slowly, and sensuously – as soon as he starts to play, and his eyes pop out of his head. Well, one of them does, but luckily you have good hand-eye co-ordination and you manage to catch it and hand it back.

You have to admit, you're even more disappointed now. Not only is he the bald, paunchy, wrinkled, badly dressed one out of Boylove, he's the bald, paunchy, wrinkled, badly dressed one with a glass eye. Why couldn't Keiran O'Reilly have come instead?

But then he winks at you with his good eye. 'Thanks for that, sweetheart,' he murmurs, and his sexy Irish voice sends chills down your spine. There's something about this faded former popstar and his close links to the music industry that's strangely attractive...

Nana Rose is clearly enjoying the set, too, dancing on the bar despite the landlord's polite requests to get off. But as soon as the music stops, she picks up her handbag to go.

'Satan needs feeding,' she announces, causing the elderly man at the next table to choke on his pint. 'Don't rush back!'

You won't. The bald one is wandering over to your table, a bottle of lager in hand.

'Hi,' you murmur. You're not sure what else to say. You used to dream about meeting one of Boylove – admittedly, not *this* one – when you were a little girl, and now it's really happening!

'Do you fancy a drink?' he asks, his sexy green eye twinkling.

You shouldn't, really. What would Dean think? But then

again, this could be a big opportunity for you! This guy knows everything there is to know about the music industry. He can answer all your questions, and give you ideas on how to break into the showbiz world.

'Red wine and coke, please,' you say shyly. 'A pint.'

Could this, you wonder, be the beginning of a financially beneficial friendship?

'...and then Roland Keating said, "That's the last time I lend anyone from Boylove my loofah!"' The bald one – whose name, and you'll be kicking yourself now, is Kyle – roars with laughter at his own story, and you can't help but join in.

You're sitting in the lounge bar of the Bull & Banker, knocking back a double Baileys and staring into Kyle's sexy green eye. You can hardly believe what's happening. Here you are, little Shampayne Sullivan, with one of the UK's leading has-beens. If only your friends from school could see you now. Oh, wait – you don't have any.

'Here,' says Kyle, patting your knee, 'drink up! I'm going to the bar. Shall I get you another?'

You're not sure where Kyle's putting the booze. He's had five pints already and has moved on to neat whisky. Maybe he's as nervous as you are?

'Sure, why not?' you murmur. The Baileys is going to your head, but you feel happy and free for the first time in ages. There's no Dean to bring you down, you can do whatever you like and Kyle does seem like the perfect guy... You glance over to where he's chatting to the barman, and he turns to you and winks.

Yes, you like him. He's charming, funny and has lots of friends in the record industry – all the things you like in a man. Sure, those pixie boots do him no favours. And his paunch is straining so hard against his T-shirt that it's threatening to escape. But you're prepared to overlook those minor niggles.

'There you go,' says Kyle, setting another Baileys on the table in front of you. 'This one's a triple – let's see if you can down it in one!'

You grasp the glass nervously. You're not really used to drinking much; Dean thinks it isn't ladylike.

'Hurry up!' urges Kyle. He knocks back his own whisky in one gulp. 'It's last orders in 10 minutes!'

Quickly, you glug down the Baileys. It burns your throat, but leaves a pleasant, warm feeling in your stomach.

Your eyes meet Kyle's. Everything else in the room seems to swim out of focus. It's no good, you've tried to resist it, but you can't fight this feeling any more: you're completely rat-arsed.

'Champagne...' he murmurs.

'It's Shampayne,' you correct him.

'Whatever.' He runs his meaty fingers over your thighs. 'I feel so lonely, sometimes, being on the road,' he says sadly.

'But you're not really on the road,' you say, puzzled. 'You told me you've got a house in the next village.'

His eye locks onto yours. 'It's just a metaphor,' he murmurs.

You've no idea what that means but he had you at 'meta...'.

You run your fingers over *his* thighs now. It's like kneading pizza dough.

'Is there anything I can do to make you feel better?' you say teasingly.

He gives a wicked, lopsided grin. 'You can Give Me Some TLC...'

You almost melt. He's quoting your favourite Boylove song.

'Babe, I don't have much time,' he croons, curling a strand of your hair around his fingers. 'I need to make you mine. I just want your company, won't you give me some TLC?'

Ten minutes later your head is banging against the taps in the women's toilets as Kyle gives you some TLC over the sink. It's like nothing you've experienced before; you feel hot all over, and there's a roaring in your ears. It's ages before you realise you've accidentally set off the handryer.

Next, you do reverse cowgirl, with Kyle sitting on the toilet. And then you both pop out for a cigarette in the car park, where you give him a hand job.

It's a magical night, and you wish it could never end but eventually you hear the landlord calling time.

'Will I see you again?' you whisper as you bend down to kiss Kyle goodbye – he's even shorter than he looked on stage.

'I'll call you,' he says, and winks.

You're finding it hard to catch your breath. Is this what they mean by starstruck? You never thought you'd get to meet a former celebrity like Kyle O'Whatsisname, at least not here, in the middle of The Countryside. Where will it all lead? But there's one thing you've forgotten: Dean. You don't want to sneak around behind his back, he's your soulmate, after all. You should probably just walk away from Kyle now, before you get too involved.

If you want to settle down with Dean, go to 4 on page 17
If you want to become Kyle's girlfriend, go to 17 on page 75

15

You're the new Kate Moss!

You're so cool, everyone wants to be your friend. You've never had any real buddies before, so it feels great to be surrounded at long last by sycophants, acolytes and hangers-on. And it's such fun hanging out with London's cool crowd. You've learnt so much from them about how to be trendy. You're embarrassed now that you ever liked the things you used to like: apparently, fish aren't cool, neither are Staffordshire Bull Terriers, and loving your granny is about as naff as you can get. You're lucky, though, because it turns out it's cool to be a Pisces, and to be 5ft 7in. Anything blue is cool, so is chocolate cake – not brownies, though – rabbits, A4 paper, having a Latvian plumber, and watching *Cash in the Attic* as long as you're wearing pop socks at the time.

You're not sure you get all the rules, and you keep making silly mistakes but you're getting there.

You're partying hard, too, hanging out in dodgy dives in

Dalston and crappy clubs in Camden. You're rubbing shoulders, and occasionally crotches when it's really crowded, with some of the trendiest celebs in London – you're forever bumping into Nick Grimshaw, Rita Ora, Cara Delevingne, Harry Styles... Who would have thought little old Shampayne Sullivan would count artists, musicians, models and It Girls among her very best fairweather friends?

Your constant drinking and drug-taking means you often turn up to modelling jobs seriously wasted, but it turns out looking and feeling like shit is cool, so no one seems to mind too much. Your career couldn't be going better, actually; you've done covers for *i-D*, *Dazed & Confused*, *Sheer* and *Caravan Monthly* – yes, it turns out caravanning is cool, too.

With so much going on, you're definitely not looking for love. But it hits you right between the eyes when you see Johnny X.

Straight away you know he's The One. Okay, you thought that about the previous Ones, but there's something different about Johnny. It could be the noughts and crosses tattoos that snake down his pale, skinny arms, which look like they were done in Biro by a nine-year-old. It might be his too-short T-shirt, which reveals a hint of ginger belly hair. Or maybe his mock Cockney accent, which he puts on even though he went to Bedales. But mostly it's that other people tell you he's cool.

You're at the bar of Camden pub, The Fox & STD, with fellow model Babyface when you spot him coming towards you. 'Wow, Johnny X! He's *thoooooo cool*!' lisps Babyface; she's only just turned six. You hand her her apple juice and salt and vinegar crisps. 'Hold these,' you whisper. 'I'm going to go and talk to him.'

'Hi there, Johnny,' you say, stepping out in front of him and flicking your hair seductively.

'Which way's the fuckin' toilets, man?', Johnny slurs.

He gives off a heady, musky scent of alcohol, sweat and wee.

'Over there,' you say, pointing towards the gents. Johnny is swaying alarmingly.

'Hey,' you say, gently touching his arm, 'are you okay?'

Johnny turns his piercing blue eyes on you; they cross, uncross, then cross again.

'Seriously, I'm off my fuckin' head...' he mutters.

Your head's all over the place, too. You can't believe that Johnny X, lead singer of The Libraryteens, is right here, talking to you. They are THE biggest UK indie band right now; they probably sell at least four, maybe five records a week.

'I loved your last single,' you tell him. 'It was cool.'

Johnny sways again. He looks like he's going to throw up. 'Yeah?' he mumbles. 'Thanks, man.'

'I'm not a man,' you say huskily. 'I'm all woman.'

Johnny puts out a shaky hand and pats your chest. 'No shit! Sorry 'bout that, dude...'

He's funny. You like this guy.

'Hey!' he says suddenly, his eyes managing to focus on you for a nanosecond. 'D'you wanna come back to mine?'

Dare you? Your previous lovers have been so clean-cut. What would it be like to bed a bad-boy rocker?

You don't get to find out, as it turns out. Not that night, or the night after, or the one after that. After taking you back to his Camberwell squat, Johnny collapses on the beer-stained sofa and declares that he's going to write a song for you. 'I'm a troubadour, a wandering poet,' he slurs, 'and you're my muse.' He picks up his guitar. 'This is gonna be called "Shampayne Supanova".'

The title sounds strangely familiar, but you don't want to spoil the mood so you don't say anything. You're not really listening anyway, to be honest, as you're more concerned that your heel has got stuck in something sticky on the carpet. It could be a huge, brown mass of chewing gum, but you suspect it might be a dead mouse.

So this is the rock 'n' roll lifestyle. You're going to have to get used to it if you want to be the girlfriend of a musical genius.

By now Johnny is sprawled out on the sofa and it seems he's out for the count, and the only other place to lie down is a mattress on the floor that looks like someone might have died on it. Reluctantly, you curl up on it in the foetal position, pulling your jacket over yourself, and hoping the mice won't come out at night and make a nest in your hair extensions.

'Night, night,' Johnny mumbles. 'Don't let the bed bugs bite.'

Unfortunately, they do. The next day your arms are covered in red lumps – they might look cool but you're not sure – you'll have to ask your cool friends. Either way, you're not going to let bed bugs put you off. You love being with Johnny. He's a dangerous, charismatic guy. He lives for partying, except on occasional weekends when he takes you back to his parents' vicarage in Gloucestershire, where he answers to Jonathan and takes you to watch the point-to-point, or for picnics at National Trust stately homes. Most days, though, he's so drunk or wasted, he's incapable of performing in the sack. And the amazing thing is, you don't actually miss sex.

At least, not with men.

You're beginning to wonder if you might be attracted to women instead. After all, 'Gay is the new black,' according to *Twatscene*. And you have to keep reinventing yourself if you want to stay cool and current. Recently you've met a couple of lesbian models and they're much more on-trend than you. Should you start batting for the other side?

Johnny, of course, doesn't seem to notice you're struggling with your sexuality. 'You inspire me, Shampayne,' he tells you one night as you're snuggling up in bed – or rather, on the mattress. 'If you left me, I wouldn't be able to write songs or poems ever again.'

It's true, Johnny seems to be at the peak of his creative powers, and the Libraryteens have been churning out new material ever since your relationship started. 'She's Got Blue Eyes' was followed by 'She's Got an Amazing Ass', then there's their biggest smash to date, 'She's Got Huge Jugs'. They're all songs about you, apparently. What would Johnny write about if you left him?

You can't decide whether to stay or go, but in the end it's Johnny who forces the decision. You get home from a *Twatscene* shoot late one night to find he's spelt out 'Let's get married!' in mouse droppings on the carpet. You're shocked, and touched. He *does* love you, and you *are* nearly twenty; maybe the time is right to settle down and become Mrs Shampayne X? It would be so cool. But then again, you have a feeling you'd be even cooler if you came out as a lipstick lesbian...

What are you going to do?

If you want to marry Johnny, go to 50 on page 210
If you want to try lipstick lesbianism, go to 5 on page 18

16

Your plastic surgery plans are on hold. Pleasing C-Rock is more important to you than achieving physical perfection.

You must have been crazy to even consider going ahead when you weigh up what you might have lost. This is the best relationship you've ever had, financially speaking. C-Rock completes you. He's your other half, your soulmate, your meal ticket, too.

'Oh, C-Rock,' you sigh, as he cradles you in his arms after another of your bizarre lovemaking sessions, 'I've never been more famous.'

C-Rock strokes your hair and gazes into your eyes.

'Then marry me and make it legal,' he whispers.

'I love you even more than my stuffed seagull...'

Sometimes you feel C-Rock might be losing his edge, lyrics-wise:

'...We'll have our nuptials in a French chateau,
And sell our wedding pictures to *Hello!*

I'll get a pre-nup drawn up by my lawyers...'

You silence C-Rock with a kiss. And not because you think the author of this book might not have been able to think of a rhyme for lawyers.

A French chateau, that's such a beautiful image! Tears spring to your eyes. Are you ready for marriage, and all that would mean? Becoming Mrs C-Rock would be a huge step. But there's currently no one else you'd rather spend the next four to five years of your life with.

'Yes,' you breathe. 'I *will* be your wife.'

C-Rock's face lights up. He pulls you, and a Beanie Baby, to his chest, and before you know it, you're making peculiar love all over again.

Your wedding is a truly spectacular affair. Brangelina, Pharrell Williams, Will Smith, Beyoncé and Jay-Z are just a few of the celebrities who can't make it, unfortunately. Neither can Barack and Michelle Obama, Cameron Diaz, Oprah Winfrey or Justin Timberlake. But you do get Derek Hough off *Dancing with the Stars* and Courtney Stodden.

The highlight of the evening is the debut of C-Rock's latest video, which is displayed on giant TV screens arranged around the marquee. It features the two of you making love as C-Rock drives a ride-on lawnmower around the garden. It's all very artistic and tastefully done; there are only two shots of C-Rock's buttocks, and you only get to see your left nipple.

Later, when your guests, the TV camera crews and the team of *Ooh La La!* photographers have left, you and C-Rock collapse into a hammock on the verandah and gaze up at the stars. Lying in the arms of this amazing man makes you feel so safe. Although remembering he could theoretically divorce you on a whim at any time and leave you virtually penniless makes you feel slightly less safe. But what the hell, for now you have everything you've ever wanted: a Grammy-award-winning (albeit kinky) husband, worldwide notoriety, a hot body and fabulous hair. Maybe, in the future, the time will be right to have a baby, and you and C-Rock can give your child a unique and tasteful name like Stickov Rock, or Sedimentary Rock, that will allow him or her to grow up with their dignity intact. But until then...

YOUR CELEBRITY ADVENTURE IS OVER

17

At first, Kyle seems like the perfect semi-famous boyfriend. His notoriety is opening all sorts of doors for you. He's better known than you realised, actually, owing to his ongoing battle with alcoholism, his acrimonious divorce and *that* 2011 incident with the Shetland pony. ('A silly misunderstanding,' according to Kyle. 'The farmer jumped to all the wrong conclusions.') What's more, the press can't seem to get enough of photos of an ageing, paunchy, faded music star out and about with his pretty, huge-breasted teenage lover. Pap shots of Kyle mauling you at the mall, groping you at the grocer's and pawing you at the pawn shop start appearing in the celebrity magazines. 'I'LL HAVE A BABY SHAM' screams the *Daily Maul* headline, above a picture of Kyle giving your butt a pat at the patisserie counter. There's no doubt about it, you're on your way to being infamous...

The only downside is Dean.

'I can't believe you've done this to me!' he screams down the phone. 'Were you just using me, 'til someone better came along? Is that it?'

Oh, Dean... He can't possibly expect to compete with Kyle – Kyle has a Subaru. But why must he be so negative?

'Can't you just be happy for me?' you plead with him. 'I've got everything I've ever wanted, and that's what matters.'

But Dean doesn't see it your way. Never mind. Within a couple of weeks you've moved out of Nana Rose's and into Kyle's seven-bed former vicarage in the next village.

'Happy, Shampers?' he asks you one rainy afternoon as you're snuggled up on his sofa in front of *Deal Or No Deal*.

'Yes, babe, you know I am,' you tell him. 'You and your industry contacts mean the world to me.'

Kyle beams. 'I can't believe how much my life has changed since I met you,' he says. 'I'm in the papers again, there's even talk of a Boylove reunion. We're a brilliant team.'

'It's a shame we're so happy,' you muse, 'otherwise we could go on *Celebrity Relationship Rehab*. We could talk about the fact that I'm only seventeen, and you're pushing fifty. You could wear a beanie hat and jeans that are clearly too young for you.'

Kyle is warming to your theme. 'And you could wear a really trashy dress, and no bra...'

'And we could both talk about karma, and "connecting", and people will think we're *really weird*...'

Just thinking about the publicity you might generate is making you horny.

'Why don't we slip out of these clothes?' you ask with a sly grin.

'But it's cold!' Kyle complains.

You run your hands over his moobs, saying, 'We can warm each other up.'

'I don't know, Shampayne, I've just had the sofa reupholstered.'

Oh, for God's sake! Since that first night at the Bull & Banker, Kyle's sex drive has taken a nosedive. Sometimes it seems he'd rather play Scrabble or browse through the Suttons Seeds catalogue than make love to you.

Kyle notices your crestfallen face. 'Oh, alright, then,' he says, reluctantly. 'You'd better fetch me my slippers first, though. My chilblains are playing up something rotten.'

Making love takes a while, as Kyle keeps having to change positions for a better view of Noel Edmonds. But after it's over, he falls into a contented doze and lies snoring gently, his stomach rising and falling like a blancmange.

You sigh. You should be delirious with happiness, just being the girlfriend of this well-connected, semi-famous man but you've been with Kyle over a month now, and he still hasn't suggested introducing you to any agents or A&R people – despite having heard your amazing singing voice. Doesn't he understand how much a music career means to you? How it's all you've ever thought, or dreamt, about since three or four weeks ago?

You'd thought he might at least have posted a few of your videos on YouTube, or made a few phone calls on your behalf. After all, didn't he say your cover of Beyoncé's 'Halo' 'was like listening to Lucy Ferr himself'? You don't know Lucy Ferr's stuff – you'd have thought he'd be a girl, with that name – but Kyle assures you you're the vocal double.

What can you do to convince Kyle that you're serious about singing? That you want to be as big as Adele? Only in terms of stardom, mind, not in dress size.

Well, if Kyle won't help you, there are only two things you can do: put some videos up on YouTube so the public can see how talented you are. OR make a sex tape and get noticed that way.

What's it to be?

If you want to concentrate on your music, go to 26 on page 111
If you'd rather release a sex tape, go to 7 on page 26

18

Vince Vole Variety's HQ is a static caravan parked out the back of Tile Supastore on the edge of the village.

'It's just temporary, while my new flagship office is being decorated,' he explains when you call in first thing on Monday morning.

Vince looks exhausted. He's still in his vest, boxer shorts and electronic curfew tag; you're guessing he's been up all night long, talent-agenting.

'First things first,' he says, as he shrugs on a dressing gown and sits down at the Formica breakfast bar. 'We need to get a marketing strategy in place.'

You look blank.

'We need to get you seen, get you noticed... You need a strong Web presence,' he explains. 'Do you tweet?'

'No, but I can whistle!'

Vince sighs. 'No, I mean, do you use Twitter? Instagram? Snapchat? YouTube? We should get some sexy selfies out there.'

Wannabe

You shake your head. So far your sexy pictures and videos have been for Dean and Dean alone, and possibly Dean's mates, knowing Dean. Tears prick your eyes as you picture Dean's pale, weasly face. Have you made the right decision? You've heard that he's already moved on, and got Tamara Harris *and* Becky Carter pregnant. It could have been you...

'Okay, let's get started,' Vince says, clapping his hands together. 'I'm going to take a few shots of you cleaning the caravan, and we'll take it from there.'

'That doesn't sound all that sexy!' you say, puzzled.

'You can do it in your bra,' Vince says, thrusting a mop and bucket into your hands.

An hour later, the caravan's sparkling, and Vince is confident he has all the shots he needs. 'These are great!' he says enthusiastically, scrolling through the pictures on his camera phone. 'I'll post them up later. Same time next week?'

You're thrilled to have taken your first steps into the world of showbiz! During the next few weeks you follow Vince's advice, and post selfies, belfies and welfies. And shelfies – shots of you putting up shelves around Nana Rose's flat. And elfies – pictures of you dressed as a pixie on your way out to a fancy-dress party. And that's not all! Vince has managed to get you some promotional work; you're 'the face' of Tattycoats mobile dog-grooming service, and you've handed out leaflets at the village fete for Suckups, a local drain specialist. And yet despite all this, the money isn't exactly rolling into your bank account. Vince pays you cash in hand after each job, and you suspect he might be creaming off more than the 75 per cent he's entitled to as your manager.

And what about your acting and singing talents? They're wasted right now. You need the world to see what else you have to offer.

'Do you think there's a chance you could get me some other types of work?' you complain one day, when you pop in to Vince's caravan to collect your 'Golf Sale: This Way' sign.

Vince's eyes suddenly go cold. He looks like Robin Thicke's older, plumper, shorter, less attractive, more annoyed brother. 'You're working non-stop, what are you complaining about?' he says gruffly.

You're a little intimidated by Vince when he's in this kind of mood, but still determined to make your point.

'I thought, maybe some TV work...'

Vince's brow furrows. 'Well, I guess there's a possibility of some reality stuff,' he says. 'It's something I've been looking into for you. Just wait a sec...'

He sits in front of his computer and punches a few keys.

'What about this?' he says, pointing at the screen.

'Contestants needed for new BBC reality show, *Tudor Country House Sex Shed*, presented by Jeremy Paxman,' you read. 'Volunteers will work to restore an Elizabethan knot garden by day, and be filmed having sex in the greenhouse by night. Their efforts will be rated by a panel of experts including Mariella Frostrup and Alan Titchmarsh.'

'I'm not sure,' you say, frowning. 'Sounds a bit middle-aged.'

'There's this one,' says Vince. '"Production company seeks up-for-anything, physically fit males and females aged eighteen to thirty to take part in *Shitty City Gang Bang*. Contestants will be parachuted into Middlesborough town centre and have to fight off muggers and sexual predators."'

'Sounds good, but I'm not eighteen for a couple of months.'

Wannabe

'Shame,' says Vince, scrolling down the page. 'Or there's this one, *Piddler on the Roof*? Nah, maybe not...'

'Does it have to be a reality show?' you ask tentatively. 'I thought maybe you could get me an audition for *Waterloo Road*, or *Holby City*?'

Vince throws his hands in the air and gives a little chuckle. 'Look, love, let's not kid ourselves,' he says. 'You're a pretty girl an' all, but you ain't exactly Dame Judi Dench.'

'Of course not!' you scoff. 'She's *ancient*!' How could Vince even think about comparing you to her? Tears prick your eyes.

Vince seems to soften. 'It's alright,' he says, more kindly, putting a consoling arm around you. 'There's always nudey stuff.'

You're shocked. 'What do you mean?'

'Not full-on porn, obviously,' he backtracks, seeing the look on your face. 'You know, topless stuff, for the lads' mags.'

Topless stuff? You're not sure. Up until now, only Dean, Nana Rose, your GP and anyone who's driven past your front garden when you're sunbathing topless – which is quite a lot of people, granted, given your house faces directly onto a main road – have seen your boobs. Parading your body for all and sundry seems such a big step. Is this the direction you really want to go in?

What should you do?

If you want to give topless modelling a try, go to 31 on page 140
If you'd rather see what else Vince has lined up for you, go to 25 on page 107

19

You've landed your first movie role! You're Third Girl on Beach in new low-budget horror *Squidnami*!

It's a speaking part as well. You get to say, 'Aaaaaaarrrrrrgh!!!' as your torso is ripped in half by the Squidnami's rapacious jaws.

'That's great, Shampayne, just keep doing that...' the director yells as you run, bouncily, along the beach, looking scared.

'The squid is out there, he's coming for you!' the director directs you. 'Now rip off your bikini top in a panic!'

You fling your bikini top at the green screen, where the Squidnami will be digitally added in later. You're putting everything you've got into this part; you're pretending really, really hard. The audience needs to feel Third Girl on Beach's pain. You've even developed a back story for her: she's a girl who's come to the beach to sunbathe.

'Aaaaarrrrrgghh!' you yell, putting as much fear into your voice as you can muster; you're imagining another tax bill coming your way. Hey, this acting thing is actually really easy!

And what do you know? 'So bad, it's good' is the critics' verdict. The film's a box-office success! All of a sudden, you're in demand.

Casting agents take you out for lunch and hit on you. Producers twice your age wine you and dine you, and hit on you. And more parts follow. You're Exotic Dancer 2 in *Earthwormquake*, Sexy Cop in *Dinostorm*, and eventually, you get to be a leading lady, climatologist Dr Rachel Hotnesse, in blockbuster *Hurricanine*.

You've cornered the market in natural-disaster/predator hybrid low-budget horror movies – you're the new Tara Reid!

Your latest movie, *Crocalanche*, is your most demanding yet. It requires moving, speaking and pretending, all at the same time. You've just filmed a scene in which you've had to flee from giant prehistoric crocodiles that have been woken from their snowy mountain lair by a bunch of teenagers on a snowboarding trip, and frankly, you're exhausted.

You flop into a heap on the velvet chaise longue in front of your trailer. No one understands how much you're suffering for your art! You snap your fingers at a runner hopping nervously from foot to foot, awaiting your next command. Your rages have become notorious, and it doesn't take much to set you off.

'Get me some sparkling water!' you demand. 'A single ice cube, one straw – it must be a red one, though. Go!'

The runner takes off.

What's the betting he fucks up, like the last one did, and brings you the wrong brand of water? You can tell your Ty Nant from your Iskilde just by sniffing them. Yes, you're turning into quite a Hollywood diva – and not before bloody time!

Wannabe

You've finally got to where you deserve to be: living the high life in LA. It's quite a step up from a council flat in The Countryside to a 5,000-sq ft condo in the Hollywood Hills. And you've done it all through luck and occasionally flashing your noo-noo. Sitting out here on your sun terrace, watching the smog lift from downtown LA, where the poor people live, you feel a sense of satisfaction. If all the haters who told you you'd never amount to anything could see you now...

You pick up your platinum-plated Tiffany breakfast spoon, ready to tuck in to your morning alpaca-milk yogurt. Wait a minute – what's going on with the pomegranate-seed topping? Your chef usually arranges the seeds into your initials, but today he hasn't bloody bothered, they're just randomly scattered. *What the bloody hell is going on?*

'Florencia!' you shout. Your elderly Hispanic housemaid comes running, or at least does her best to. Her arthritic hips make little clicking sounds.

'*Si*, Miss Shampayne?' she pants. She's scanning your face to see what's wrong. Unfortunately, since your last Botox injection you only have one expression.

'I'm furious!' you explain.

'Ah!' she says, nodding fervently. '*Si, si.* What is wrong, Miss Shampayne? Did I not iron the toilet paper the way you like it?'

'No, no, that's not it,' you mutter irritably. 'You got the creases down the middle just perfectly.'

Florencia visibly relaxes.

'It's my yogurt,' you explain. 'I can't eat it.' You push the bowl away. 'It's all... *wrong*!' You don't deserve this on a Tuesday. Tears of frustration well up in your eyes. 'Why is it so *fucking hard* for people to get things right now and again?'

Florencia just stares at you, wide-eyed. She obviously can't believe this monumental fuck-up *has actually happened* either.

The tears are coming hard and fast now. Why can't people get things right? You fling yourself out of the chair and onto the polished marble floor, and lie face down, weeping bitter tears. 'All I'm asking for is a little attention to detail!' you screech, tears coursing down your cheeks. 'Fuck! Fuck! *Fuck*!!!!!'

'Shall I fetch the doctor, Miss Shampayne?' Florencia asks nervously.

'I don't need a fucking doctor, I need my pomegranate seeds arranged properly!' You pound the floor with your fist. 'Make! It! Happen!'

'*Si, si....*' You hear a scraping sound as Florencia gathers up the breakfast things, then her scuttling footsteps as she hurries downstairs, towards the nearest of your five kitchens.

Jesus, it's exhausting sometimes, being you. People are constantly letting you down. It's unfair that you have a reputation for being 'difficult', when actually you just have high standards. What's so demanding about wanting your air filtered and infused with the scent of lemons before you breathe it? That's just basic, everyday stuff. Sure, there was a time when none of this would have mattered to you but back then, you didn't know any better. Back then, you were just a clueless wannabe.

You're conscious that no one has come to pick you up off the floor yet. Hasn't Florencia told the pool boys you need help? Are you supposed to get *yourself* back into your chair? *What the fuck are you paying these people for?*

Well, you're just going to lie here until someone comes and sorts this mess out. Even if it takes seven hours and you have to lie here in your own wee. Even if it takes seven days and involves you actually starving to death. It would be worth it to teach your so-called staff a lesson.

Yes, you've finally found a cause worth dying for: you.

YOUR CELEBRITY ADVENTURE IS OVER

20

With your new JJ breasts, your glamour career is on the up and up. You're a regular in the lads' mags and on page 5 of *The Bun*. There's a real buzz about you, and it's not just because you've started bee-keeping in your spare time.

But even though things are going great for you, you still can't get over your spat with Lacey Lamberton. How dare she treat you that way? You're not just anyone, you're Shampayne Sullivan!

You seize every opportunity that comes your way to get back at her. Lacey carries a chihuahua in her designer handbag so you get a lamb and cart it around in a shopping trolley studded with Swarovski crystals. Lacey gets 3-inch shellac nail extensions, you get komodo-dragon claws grafted onto your hands. Lacey gets a new rose tattoo on her thigh so you have your entire backside decorated with flowers. You'd think it might look tacky but actually it's an assterpiece.

Wannabe

It's clear your rivalry is getting out of hand. But when Lacey's abroad on a calendar shoot you get your chance to best her once and for all when you bump into her fiancé, Dutch footballer Neyan Der Thal, in his hotel bedroom at the Manchester Grand.

'Oh, hi, Neyan!' you say, emerging from his bathroom wearing just a fluffy towel and a smile. 'I thought you might be feeling lonely now Lacey's out of town.'

Neyan's lumpen, heavy-set face wears an expression of shock. His mouth opens and closes noiselessly; his beetle brows furrow. Now you're looking at him close up, you can see why his nickname is The Caveman.

You let the towel drop to the floor.

'I'm a very naughty girl,' you coo. 'And I need to be punished!'

That seems to do the trick. You and Neyan are grappling on the floor in seconds. 'Oh, Neyan,' you croon into his ear, 'I've dreamt of this moment since an hour or so ago.' You may have to close your eyes so you can forget you're making love with the Missing Link, but sex with Neyan is surprisingly good. Uninhibited and wild, he roars like a lion. He hoots like a gibbon. He makes funny little snorty noises like you imagine an aardvark might make. You've never had such animalistic sex. Afterwards he even uses his back leg to scratch behind his ear.

'Oh, Neyan, that was amazing,' you sigh, falling back, exhausted, on the pillow.

Neyan looks down at you and smiles. 'Man, woman, make love, good,' he mutters approvingly. His English really could do with some work.

And you can't resist. 'Am I better than Lacey?' you ask, pouting seductively.

Neyan looks worried. 'Woman keep secret. No speak Lacey.'

Wannabe

'It's okay, baby,' you assure him. 'This is just between me and you.'

Neyan leans over and tries to gently stroke your hair; a clump comes out in his hand. 'We do soon? Again?' he asks hopefully.

You shrug. You're going to play hard to get… although you admit it's a bit late now. 'I'll have to check my schedule,' you say coolly.

Neyan puts his fist in his mouth and starts gnawing his knuckles.

'Look,' you sigh, 'why don't you call me when Lacey's out of town again?'

His face brightens at that; he looks almost homosapien. 'Good, good! Neyan happy!' he says, nodding furiously and slapping his chest.

After that, it's only a matter of time before Lacey finds out about you and Neyan. You help things along by leaving your thong in his glove compartment, sending nude selfies to his phone, and posting cryptic little tweets such as 'Got shagged senseless by Neyan Der Thal this arvo #cheatingonLacey', but she still doesn't cotton on straight away.

The crunch comes one lunchtime when you're at Neyan and Lacey's penthouse apartment. Lacey's safely out of the way, at a Hair Pilates workshop. You and Neyan are dry-humping in the hot tub; you'd both prefer to be wet-humping, but Neyan's housekeeper must have forgotten to refill the tub that morning.

'What the *hell*?!!'

You both turn in the direction of the voice. OMG, it's Lacey! She wasn't due back until later. This is awful. You didn't want Lacey to find out this way.

Oh, who are you kidding? Of course you did.

Wannabe

Neyan is the first to react. 'No what look like!', he says pathetically, jumping out of the tub and grabbing a towel to cover his embarrassment.

'Not what it *looks like*?' Lacey screeches. Her face is screwed up with hatred. She points an expensively manicured finger at you, and makes jabbing motions. 'I'll tell you what it looks like. It looks like *there's some dirt in the pool*!'

Is she talking about you, or referring to some *real* dirt? You find metaphors really confusing...

'Get rid of her!' Lacey yells at Neyan. 'I want this slapper out of my house!' She turns back towards you. 'And you – if I ever, *ever* catch you talking to, or even looking at my fiancé again...'

Fiancé? She's planning on *marrying* him after this? And after last month's rent-boy scandal? On top of last year's horsemeat-dealing and orphans'-Christmas-present-stealing scandals? How does Lacey find it in her heart to keep forgiving the £60,000-a-week striker?

'Oh yeah?' you retort. 'Well, I don't need *your* stupid fiancé. I've got one of my own!'

You're not sure why you said that, you *don't* have one but you're pretty sure you can get one from somewhere.

'Yeah, I'm getting married next month!' you sneer. 'And I'm going to have a 12-foot train and ride into the ceremony on a white horse.'

'Oh really?' Lacey retorts. 'My train is 20ft long, and I'm riding in on a unicorn.'

'But my horse is going to have golden hooves, and it's going to shoot rose petals out of its ass,' you counter.

'My unicorn's got wings, and it's going to take guests for sky-rides on its back,' Lacey shoots back. 'Oh, and by the way, I'm pregnant.'

'I'm pregnant, too!' you blurt out. 'And I'm having twins!'

Neyan's jaw hits the floor. Lacey's fist strikes Neyan.

'You bloody idiot!' she shrieks. 'Didn't you use protection?'

Of course you're *not* pregnant, and you're not getting married either but now you've landed yourself in an awkward position. There's no way Lacey is getting one over on you. You're either going to have to find some kids, or a fiancé, at short notice.

It can't be too hard, can it?

If you want to find a fiancé, and quick, go to 12 on page 50

If you want to pick up a couple of kids from the shops, go to 48 on page 199

21

You can't seem to stop yourself. The sight of Lacey's retreating back is like a red rag to a bull.

'Hey, slapper!' you yell.

Lacey turns around.

'Well, at least you know your name,' you sneer.

Lacey's eyebrows shoot up towards the ceiling. She can hardly believe you've dared to speak to her, let alone insult her. 'Are you talking to *me*?' she says coldly.

The room has gone deadly quiet; the make-up girls are open-mouthed. This is the first time anyone has ever insulted the great Lacey Lamberton.

You stand motionless, sizing Lacey up. She's probably a 34-inch chest, a 22-inch waist, with 35, or possibly 36-inch hips. You're really good at sizing people up, it's one of your strengths.

'Yeah,' you say. 'I *am* talking to you.'

Lacey takes a step towards you. She's itching to slap you, you can tell, but is probably more worried about her manicure.

'Well, well,' she says, her upper lip curling up into a sneer. 'You really think you're something, don't you? Let me tell you, sweetheart – you're *nothing*.'

'Come on, girls,' Linda interjects. 'There's no need for this, let's all be friends.'

'You've done, what, one little shoot?' Lacey says, stabbing her fingertip in your face. 'Do you know how many I've done?'

'Twenty?' you guess.

'More!'

'Thirty?'

'Higher!'

'I don't know, 400?'

'Not that many, you stupid tart.'

'One hundred and fifty?'

'Close. I've done *130* shoots, and there's nothing I don't know about the glamour business. I know all the photographers, all the agents, all the magazine editors, and if I tell them not to use some jumped-up little piece of trash, well…. Let's just say, this first shoot was your last.'

'But the thing is, I'm only just eighteen,' you say coolly. 'You're almost twenty-two. Face it, you're past it. And your boobs are starting to sag.'

That seems to be the final straw for Lacey. Carefully, she sets down her Mulberry bag, removes her diamanté hoop earrings and takes a step towards you. You square up to her. Although you're standing a foot and a half apart, your boobs are touching. It's weirdly erotic.

She flicks her hair back out of her face. 'Bring it, then,' she says. And before you know what's happening, you and Lacey are wrestling on the ground, pulling out handfuls of each other's hair extensions. Your robe has fallen open so everyone can see your bits and pieces. Lacey is kicking your shins with her pointy Jimmy Choo boots and twisting your nipples. You manage to grab hold of her belly button ring and give it a sharp tug. Lacey shrieks in pain. Then her face twists into a snarl and she reaches out and scratches at your eyes.

'Not the bloody eyelash extensions!' you scream. 'I only just had them done!'

'Tough!' Lacey rips off your left falsie.

'This is brilliant, girls!' shouts Linda, who's snapping away in the background. 'Shampayne, can you twist round a bit so we can see more of your bum?'

By this time you've got Lacey pinned to the floor, and are pummelling her boobs with your fists.

'Don't! They'll burst!' Lacey yells.

'Do you give in?' you shout. You're exhausted, frankly.

'Alright, just get off!'

You climb off Lacey's prone body and stand up. You're just in your thong now and the lighting assistant and the traffic warden, who's still here, are gaping at you, open-mouthed.

'Jesus, you're a cyclepath!' Lacey shouts, scrambling to her feet. The floor is littered with clumps of fake hair and vajazzle sequins. 'Linda, tell this freak to get out!'

'Now, let's not be hasty,' Linda says, putting an arm around Lacey. 'Why don't we have a cup of tea and look at the shots first, before we make any rash decisions?'

You and Lacey have made the front page of the *Daily Maul*.

'SHAMMI-LAMBY DING DONG!' screams the headline, above a huge picture of you and Lacey wrestling half-naked on the floor.

'The claws were out when glamour girl Lacey Lamberton met newcomer Shampayne Sullivan,' reads the copy. 'Words were exchanged between the two topless models yesterday at the West London studio of photographer Linda Lovely, and before long, the girls had ripped off each other's clothes and were involved in a semi-naked catfight.'

Your boobs look great, it was a good angle for you. Lacey, on the other hand, looks decidedly droopy. Yes, there's no doubt about it, you've come out of this on top. And like your boobs, your career is looking perky! You've landed a contract with men's weekly, *Monkeyballz*. *The Bun* wants you to be a regular Page 5 Girl. You've even done your own calendar. And people are starting to recognise you wherever you go. You should be on top of the world, but for one thing: you still haven't shagged a footballer.

You can't really call yourself a success until you've slept with at least one Premier-League player. You might have the best breasts, the most fabulous hair, but without footballer-shagging, it counts for nothing. Alex Gerrard, Coleen Rooney... Both started by shagging footballers, and now they've got their own perfumes! And Abbey Clancy shagged Peter Crouch, then won *Strictly Come Dancing*!

'Stop moaning, then, and get out there!' Nana Rose says encouragingly. 'Those A-list players aren't going to shag themselves.' She pauses for a moment. 'Well, I suppose I wouldn't put it past them...'

Nana Rose is right, as usual. You're not going to meet anyone lying around at home in your lingerie. You should hit the town in your lingerie!

So that's exactly what you do. And it turns out to be a great decision. Half the Ladchester team are out tonight, in the VIP section of Tiger Tiger. You're wearing an eye-catching ensemble of fishnet tights, bra and teensy satin knickers, so you're not surprised when Darren Doyle, Ladchester's star striker, notices you. And not before time – you've been straddling him for at least 20 minutes and your inner thighs are getting chafed.

Darren pours you the last glass from a bottle of champagne.

'Shall I order another magnum?' he asks, clicking his fingers to attract the maître d's attention.

'Oooh, can you get me one, too?' you ask. 'Double Caramel, please, they're the best.'

He smiles. 'Sure!'

What a gent! His wife is one lucky lady.

It's a fantastic night. You dance. You pout. You flick your hair around a lot. You sit on Darren's lap. Darren sits on *your* lap. You pout a bit more. Darren flicks your hair around. You flick Darren's hair around…

By 2am you're a bit tipsy after your five glasses of champagne, two WKDs, four rum and cokes and a bottle of neat Bourbon. But Ladchester team captain Sol Baxter is more than that – he's totally wasted.

'Why don't you come back to the hotel with us, Shammi?' he leers, stumbling towards your table. 'You, me and Darren – we could have a spit roast.'

It's tempting – you are a bit peckish after all. But a barbecue? At this hour? You're not sure you could manage it.

'What about a room-service ham and cheese toastie instead?' you ask.

Sol looks baffled. 'A ham and cheese toastie? I don't think I've ever tried that but I'm game if you are!'

It's settled, then. You'll pop back to the players' hotel for a chat, a snack and maybe a game of charades.

'Darren didn't mess around. As soon as we were alone he stripped off to his tight white underpants. I wasn't all that impressed with his body, to be honest. He has muscly legs, but his top half wasn't all that well developed. I like huge biceps, and his were just average. I also noticed he had a few pimples on his bum.

'Darren lay on the bed and asked me to get naked, too. I'm not that sort of girl so I said no – I just took off my bra but kept my knickers on, and performed a sex act on him. For a while afterwards we just lay there, chatting a bit about the new Ferrari that he'd just bought, and about his wife Sienna and the kids; he didn't seem guilty that he was cheating on her. But he said it wasn't disloyal as long as I faced the wall and he didn't look into my eyes.

'He kept saying I had a really beautiful body, and that he really liked me. Then we had sex five times. Darren had good stamina, as you'd expect from a footballer, but he talked all the way through. I usually like talking dirty, but with Darren it was all football stuff, like, "Get in, my son!" and "Back of the net!", which was a bit of a turn-off, if I'm honest.

'I'd give Darren 6 out of 10 in bed. He put a lot of effort in but his manhood was a bit on the small side.

'Afterwards, he said he'd see me around, and gave me a peck on the cheek. But now I realise he was just using me for sex. I feel dirty and ashamed. I really thought he loved me.'

You can't believe it – the front page of *The Bun* is all about *you*! 'GLAMOUR MODEL SHAMPAYNE SCORES WITH LADCHESTER STRIKER DARREN DOYLE,' you read.

Where did they get this stuff from? Oh, that's right, from *you*.

Just then, your phone rings. Well, to tell the truth, it doesn't ring *exactly* then; it rings some time after you'd read the rest of the paper, had a poo, showered, dressed, flicked through the Next catalogue and had a coffee. But for the sake of dramatic tension, just then, your phone rings.

It's Darren.

'I can't believe you did this!' he rages. 'I trusted you, but you're nothing but a cheap slapper!'

Tears fill your eyes. He's got you all wrong, you're a *very expensive* slapper.

'Don't be like that, Darren,' you plead. 'We could have been so good together!'

'My wife is talking about divorcing me. I never want to see you, or talk to you ever again!' he screams. The phone goes dead.

You collapse onto your bed in tears. Darren was the perfect man, and now everything is ruined.

You sit up again. Oh well, never mind. Onwards and upwards! You're due at the opening of Sellsfridges' new nail bar in an hour. Better get to the tanning salon!

If you still want to take your glamour career to the next level, go to 28 on page 122

If you want to take a break from the relentless smut and innuendo, go to 56 on page 231, where you'll find a gorgeous picture of some kittens

22

You've tabbed for ten clicks under the searing desert sun, with a full 60lb Bergen, when it hits you: you've strayed into the wrong book. But right now there's no time for regrets.

'Incoming!' yells Thommo, as bullets thud into the sand, just yards ahead. Jesus, there's zero cover out here. Where the hell *is* the bastard?

You hit the dirt.

'Shit, they got me!' It's Jacko's voice. He's lying about six feet away, to your left. You shuffle on your elbows towards him.

'You'll be alright, you Welsh bastard,' you assure him. 'Just hang on.'

'I think it's serious, mate,' Jacko gasps. He's panicking. 'I can't bloody feel my legs!'

He's bleeding out, the sand beneath him turning a deep vermilion.

'Thommo!' you yell. 'Jacko's hit! We need Medevac.'

Wannabe

'Ain't gonna happen,' Thommo calls back. 'We gotta move him to the extraction point.'

'But that's another two clicks away!'

'Leave me!' Jacko yells. 'Just get the fuck out of here!' You can tell the Big Man's in pain. 'Shampayne – wait!' He grabs your hand and squeezes it. 'I just gotta say it, I'll never get the chance, now...' Jacko's voice is getting fainter.

'What is it, you big hairy bastard?' You bend down, so your ear is just above Jacko's mouth.

'I don't know how to say this, so I'll just say it.' Jacko grimaces in pain. 'I've always found you attractive, Shampayne. You're different to the other guys.'

Funny, you're not even shocked – you guess you've always known it.

'Is it because of the tits?' you ask gently.

He gives a strangled sigh, struggling to get his breath now.

'They are bloody fantastic, mate,' he rasps, trying hard to smile.

'Don't talk now, Jacko,' you say. 'I'm gonna get you out of here.'

Rounds from the insurgents' AK47s are zipping and cracking over your heads.

'Nah, mate, I'm done. Get moving. I'm just gonna lie here and check out your arse as you run.'

'We need to move out – now!' Thommo's voice is urgent. The enemy fire is becoming more insistent.

Quickly, you bend and kiss Jacko's parched lips. Then you punch him in the balls, for old time's sake.

'No waaaaaaay!' you say quietly.

Jacko gives a faint smile. 'No waaaaaaay!' he whispers back.

Then he's gone.

Wannabe

You can't believe it. Jacko's always been there, since Alpha platoon. The team won't be the same without him. He's...

Wait a minute, have you broken *another* nail? Jesus, yes, you have! It's hanging on by a thread. Your body turns cold and a wave of nausea hits you. 'Medevac, I need Medevac!' you shriek, clutching your injured hand.

Fuck this crazy war! And fuck this godforsaken desert! You want out of here. You want to go shopping at Bluewater. You want to hang out at Mahiki and see if you can pull a Premier-League footballer. You want a proper Céline bag instead of this shitty Army standard-issue rucksack. You want to go back to the other book! But it's too late now...

YOUR CELEBRITY ADVENTURE IS OVER

23

Well, apparently you *can't* be a teacher. You 'need more than one GCSE in Nail Art Technology to qualify for training'. Who knew?

Oh well, back to the day job at 37 on page 157

24

You finish your tower of meringues with a sprinkling of crystallised rose petals, then step back to admire your handiwork.

Ta-da! They look incredible – the perfect centrepiece for the shop window. You hope it's all been worth it. It was a big risk, leaving your Battersea flat and your busy job as a PR for a handbag firm, to come to Tinychester to open a cake shop. But after Daniel walked out on you, your confidence was at rock bottom and you needed a project, something just for you. Hence, Shammi's Sweet Treats.

The sign above the door looks wonderfully inviting: shiny gold lettering against a tasteful eau de nil background, with tiny sprigs of flowers adding a feminine flourish. It's lovely.

You're lovely, too. You have lovely shiny hair and lovely eyes. And you're built like a blow-up doll. No wonder all the eligible men in Tinychester have been queuing up to meet you. Roger the vicar must have popped in at least three times yesterday to see how you're getting on, and you've caught surly-yet-sexy farmhand

Abel staring at you through the shop window on his way to and from work. But it's hunky vet Luke who's caught your eye.

And talk of the devil, he's coming this way!

Quickly, you whip off your Shammi's Sweet Treats apron and smooth down the creases in your Cath Kidston tea dress.

Just a minute, your *what*? What the *fuck* are you wearing? A *tea dress*? You look like a *freakin' granny*! Then you twig what's happened: you've strayed into a badly written chick-lit book. *OMG, this is a bloody disaster!*

Too late now, here comes Luke. Hastily, you undo the top four buttons of your dress and lean provocatively over the counter. You just have time to grab a cake pop from the display case and start sucking it noisily.

'Um, hi there!' Luke says, blushing a little. He doesn't seem to know where to look. 'I wondered if you had any more of those, er, delicious cherry bakewell tarts?'

You swirl your tongue around the cake pop and look up at him with come-to-bed eyes.

'You're in luck,' you murmur, undoing one more button. 'I was just about to whip them out.'

Luke's sexy brown eyes widen in alarm.

'They're in the oven,' you explain. 'Give me a moment.'

You sway into the back room, giving a little wiggle as you bend over to open the oven door. Luke seems to be having a coughing fit. You sashay back with a tray of freshly baked tarts, golden and puffed up like pillows; they smell incredible.

Luke hesitates.

'You can feel them if you like,' you invite him. 'Go on, they're nice and firm.'

He looks nervous.

'Look, Shammi, I guess I should be upfront with you,' he says, shifting awkwardly from one foot to the other. 'I really like you. I've not been divorced long but I think I want to get to know you better. To see where things lead.'

'There's something you should know about me, too,' you say, raising your blue eyes to meet his soulful brown ones.

'There's no need,' Luke murmurs, laying his huge, tanned hand over yours. 'I think I already know what you're going to say: you've been hurt badly in the past, you're not sure whether you can give your heart away again.'

'No, it's not that,' you say, still gazing up at him. 'I was going to say, I can suck a golf ball through 20 feet of garden hose.'

Luke whips his hand away. 'Er, that's, um, super,' he says in a strangled voice. 'Well, I really must be popping back to the Jenkins' farm. I, um... one of their cows is calving.'

'Wait!' you cry as he makes a dash for the door. 'You've forgotten your tarts!' But all you can see is his muscular back and long legs as he sprints towards his Land Rover.

Honestly, what a loser! Is *everyone* in this town gay, or what? This place needs shaking up. And you, Shampayne Sullivan, are just the woman to do it. Languidly, you pick up your mobile phone and dial the number of the local paper.

'You'd better send a photographer over to Shammi's Sweet Treats,' you tell the newsdesk. 'There's a woman in the window wearing nothing but a pair of custard tarts...'

YOUR CELEBRITY ADVENTURE IS OVER

25

Vince has incredible news! He sent off a video of you dancing around in your pants to a production company, and they've offered you a place on *Monkey Business*, the new reality show they're making for Channel 5.

You and a team of other photogenic sixteen- to thirty-year-olds will be competing against a troupe of capuchins in a series of entrepreneurial tasks. The show is to be fronted by multimillionaire company owner Colin Sweetstuff, who's notorious for his brusque manner and love of plain speaking. You're pretty nervous, given that you don't know the first thing about business, but whatever happens, you're going to give it 110 per cent and reach for the skies because you're a winner with a capital W, and you dine on success sandwiches every day. And anyway, how hard can it be to beat a troupe of monkeys?

The other cast members seem nice enough: there's 'first-class graduate from the School of Charisma' Dazza, 'the world's toughest negotiator' Gazza, and Bazza, who is 'like Napoleon, Winston Churchill and Muhammad Ali rolled into one'. Then there's the girls: sales manager Abi, personal trainer Tabbi, and Flabbi, who's the token size-14 one. You're going to be living together in the monkey enclosure at Countryshire Zoo, which means you won't be able to take your hair straighteners, but you're still incredibly excited. You can hardly believe this is happening! At last, here's your chance to get out of The Countryside and start to make your mark in the showbiz world!

The only downside is that the capuchin enclosure, where your tent has been pitched, smells horrible; there's monkey poo everywhere you look. And the cameras are turned on 24 hours a day, so there's no privacy. That's a shame, because you've definitely got the hots for Bazza. He's just the way you like your men: blond, surfer-dude shaggy hair, ripped abs and an IQ lower than his inside-leg measurement. Plus, he likes Liquorice Allsorts. You like Liquorice Allsorts, too. You've got a real connection.

You're glad you've found a soulmate, because *Monkey Business* is hard going at first. For task number one you have to collect uneaten fruit from around the enclosure to make into smoothies to sell to the public. The capuchins really seem to have the edge; they've divided themselves into two sub-working groups, one concentrating on processing and the other on marketing, while you, Bazza and the others are still trying to come up with a team name. By the time you decide on Team Biscuits ('because we all like biscuits'), the monkeys have made £567.

'You're a blahdy shambles!' Lord Sweetstuff tells you. 'Them capuchins ran rings around you! I can't tell who's the blahdy monkeys and who's the professionals...'

The monkeys are thrilled with their first taste of success,

chattering noisily and flinging faeces and fruit peelings at you. The boardroom's a mess.

Thank God for Bazza! He's brought his bench press into the monkey enclosure as his luxury item, and you take to sitting up late together in front of the campfire, chatting and working out.

But then disaster strikes. By the time of your fourth task – marketing a 'green' vehicle fuelled by monkey poo – the atmosphere in the enclosure is becoming tense. It transpires that Abi and Tabbi have been sneaking extra bananas from the daily allowance, and to say the capuchins aren't happy is an understatement. Bazza isn't helping the atmosphere by doing chin-ups from the monkeys' favourite tree, running around gibbering, and beating his naked chest.

'I'm the leading salesperson of my generation!' he howls, throwing a piece of coconut shell at a wiry-looking monkey with a white stripe down his back. 'I put the "go" in negotiate...'

Suddenly, the monkey seems to crack. With a shriek, it lunges forward and with one snapping motion, sinks its sharp little teeth into Bazza's manhood.

All hell breaks loose. Zoo officials rush in with tranquiliser guns and fire off shots into the monkey's back; the emergency medical team attempt to stem Bazza's blood loss... He's in shock and has gone deathly pale. Which is a real shame, you think, because he doesn't look so hot now. You like your men tanned. And with a functioning penis.

Worse still, the show's producers decide to shut down filming on *Monkey Business* with immediate effect. They're worried about negative publicity, apparently. 'This would never have happened on *Springwatch*,' you hear one of the production assistants mutter.

What are you supposed to do now? It seems the show won't

even be broadcast on one of the cable channels, though as it turns out, footage of Bazza's monkey assault somehow finds its way onto YouTube and is viewed 900,000 times the first day it's posted, making Bazza an Internet sensation. Next thing you hear he's producing and starring in his own 'Willy Wonky' series of porn films.

You're so disappointed. Your big break, and it's all come to nothing.

'Look, I keep telling you, there's always nudey stuff,' Vince consoles you. 'You could really go places with that.'

It's true – it would be well paid, and you'd almost certainly get to shag a footballer. But part of you is still holding out for some acting work. You want to be one of the foremost actresses of your generation, another Megan Fox or Tara Reid. Should you keep trying to get your big break? Or give up and take your top, and possibly your pants, off?

Decisions, decisions...

If you want to hold out for acting work, go to 45 on page 186
If you want to give glamour work a try, go to 31 on page 140

26

It's too late to go back now – your video is up on YouTube for everyone to see.

You're singing your own composition, 'We Are Never, Ever, Ever, Ever, Ever, Ever Getting Back Together'. It's a bit like the Taylor Swift song but different in that there's a few extra 'evers' in there somewhere and you're singing it to the tune of 'London's Burning'. Amazingly, your version has already had 400,000 hits more than hers. It can't just be because you're performing in the nude...

You got Nana Rose to film the video so the camera work's a bit shaky, but all in all you're pretty pleased with the result. It doesn't really showcase your full vocal talents – those high Cs of yours that can shatter nerves – but it's a start.

You've written some other songs you think will appeal to a female audience, too. There's 'Thank God, I'm Not Pregnant, It Was Just Indigestion' and 'My Ex-Boyfriend Had a Teeny Tiny

Penis', for which you've borrowed the melody for 'The Good Ship Sails on the Ally-Ally-Oh'.

Not all the YouTube comments are flattering, but then they'll always be haters. 'Listening to this makes me want to cut off my ears and feed them to my dogs,' says some loser called Calvin Harris – but what does he know? But it's not all negative. You feel you're inspiring a new generation of girls to want to be better people. 'This makes me want to die,' someone called WandaT has written, with lots of sad-face emoticons. She's missed the 't' off 'diet', the silly moo, but it's nice that she thinks you're in good shape.

'Fantastic looking, but a voice like a scalded cat,' another post reads. 'She'd probably be great in a girlband, though.'

Actually, that's not a bad idea! If you were in a group with three or four average-looking girls – especially if one of them was downright chubby – you'd look even hotter! Right, you'd better get to London and do a few auditions...

OMG, you're auditioning for a new girlband called Chix! Just like that!

Media mogul Gideon Baxter seems to warm to you from the start.

'Give it everything you've got, Shampayne,' he says encouragingly, as you gyrate around his desk to 'I'm Sexy and I Know It'. 'Really open up, I want to see your potential.'

Cheeky sod! You usually make guys wait at least three weeks before you let them get a glimpse of that.

Gideon looks particularly impressed by your rendition of 'My Heart Will Go On' – his jaw is practically on the floor. 'There's always Auto-tune,' you hear him murmur to his assistant. It must be a second band he's putting together. Perhaps if you don't qualify for Chix, you'll make it into that one.

The other girls auditioning are just as nervous as you. 'They'll never pick both of us, our hair's too similar,' says a pinched-face girl with blonde extensions. 'They need a balance of girls. You know, a ginger one, a brunette, a curly-haired one...'

'It's true, they'll want girls with different looks,' says a pretty Asian girl, 'and different personalities.'

'Like Old Spice, Five-Spice and Spice Rack from the Spice Girls,' the blonde adds helpfully.

'Which one was Spice Rack?' You get them all muddled up.

'The one with the boobs.'

'Of course...' You all nod knowingly.

You reckon it's in the bag if they're looking for a Spice Rack for this group – you've certainly got the proportions – the other blonde is flatter than an ironing board.

You can't take anything for granted, though. You give it your all – you sing, you dance, you pout, you pout some more, until you collapse, exhausted, into Gideon's lap.

'Okay, we've reached a decision!' Gideon beams. 'Lulu, Hollie, Carly and Shampayne, stay behind, please. Everyone else can go.'

The other blonde files out with the rest of the hopefuls, looking dejected.

Wow! This has got to be good news!

Gideon gathers you together. 'Congratulations, girls, you've made it into Chix. You're going to be the next big thing!'

You can't actually believe you won a place. Even you have to admit that most of the other girls were much better singers than you. It's a mystery why that 19-stone girl with alopecia and a harelip didn't get in and you did – she sounded like Beyoncé. You think it was probably your energy that got you noticed. That, and the fact you did the whole audition in just your bra and pants.

You squeal and jump up and down with excitement. 'We've got to have Chick-names!' you say. 'Who's going first?'

Lulu, who's sweet-looking and just 5ft tall, decides to be Chick Next Door. Hollie wants to be Crazy Chick. Carly settles on Chick Norris, because she's hard.

'I could be Sexy Chick,' you suggest.

'I see you as more of a Mega-Value Deep-Fried Chicken Bucket,' says Carly. 'No offence.'

'I'll be Chicken Breasts, then,' you say, by way of compromise. You don't want to fall out with these girls – they could be the first female friends you've ever had.

Gideon is pulling out all the stops for Chix, and using all his showbiz connections. For your debut single, you're going to be working with legendary producer Sylvesta-a-a. He's flying in from LA in a week and you'll head straight for the studio to record the track. Until then, you'll be staying at a West London flat that Gideon has set up for you, which has live-action cameras in all the rooms to record footage for a documentary about the making of the band. You're all going to hang out there in the hot tub and swap bras.

'You'll be like The Saturdays, but with fewer clothes,' Gideon explains.

As it turns out, living in Acton with the girls is fantastic fun; you're really bonding as a band. Gideon suggests you have pillow fights in your underwear every night, and they're a brilliant laugh. There's no bitchiness at all although you're all secretly a bit worried about how many lines of the song – and how much press attention – you'll each be getting. Who'll be the Harry Styles of the band, and who'll be the Lewis Tomkinson?

Having girlfriends is *so* amazing. You, Carly, Hollie and Lulu go shopping together, drink together, go clubbing, share clothes and tell each other all your secrets.

'Chix rule!' is your motto. 'We'll always be BFFs, won't we, girls?' says Carly one night as you're painting each other's toenails. You're all exhausted after your last pillow fight, which as usual Carly won by stuffing her pillowcase with bricks. That's your only, teeny-weeny criticism of her: she can sometimes be a little bit competitive.

'Of course, we'll be friends forever!' says Lulu, making a heart sign with her hands. 'You guys complete me!'

This brings tears to your eyes. 'Girls, you're like sisters to me,' you say, fighting back sobs. 'Whatever happens, we'll always be there for each other.'

That slag Carly! She stole your ooohs!

Your first single is called 'Oooh!'

You've got four 'ooohs', Lulu and Hollie have three each, but Carly has five 'ooohs' and all the rest of the words. The cow! You always knew she was a backstabbing bitch.

Gideon and Sylvesta-a-a have picked Carly to be the main vocalist for your first live performance, at the annual 'London Rocks!' festival. Which means she'll get the pick of the outfits – again. At yesterday's *Poptastic!* magazine photoshoot you almost came to blows over a pair of diamanté hotpants.

True to form, today Carly snatches the orange boob tube you've got your eye on.

Wannabe

'I think I should wear that, it matches my hair,' says Carly fiercely.

'But it matches *my* skin tone!' you protest, gripping the fabric tightly with your fingers. Hell, you might even be prepared to break a nail for this!

Carly gives the top a tug. 'Let go, Shampayne, you stupid tart!'

'No, *you* let go, you silly bitch!' you retort.

Your stylist, T-Bag, comes in to break things up.

'Ladies, ladies, please calm down!' he says, wresting the top from your grasp. 'Shampayne, let Carly wear the top. I have something special lined up for you.'

That sounds promising. 'Something special?'

'Sure, I've just been to a *fabulous* vintage sale.'

Oooh, you love vintage! It's *so* much more classy than second-hand, or just plain old, stuff!

'I bought a job-lot of stage costumes from Kajagoogoo's UK tour in '83,' T-Bag explains. 'There are a couple of things I think will really suit you.'

He rifles through the clothes rail at the back of the room and pulls out a pair of gold knickerbockers and a frilly granny shirt – *what the fuck*??

'You'll rock this look!' T-Bag assures you. 'It's Lady Di meets Adam Ant.'

Carly giggles. Lulu and Hollie just looked stunned.

'I'm not wearing that!' you protest. 'It won''t show off my assets!'

T-Bag looks annoyed. 'I thought you might want to try something edgy,' he complains. 'I thought you were fashion-forward, like Victoria Beckham.'

'I *am* fashion-forward!' you protest.

'Then at least try it on.'

You snatch the knickerbockers and the shirt from T-Bag's outstretched hands, and stalk off to the toilets.

Come on, Shampayne, you think to yourself, you can make this work; you're creative. Didn't you used to customise your school uniform by just wearing a shirt and tie some days, and leaving your skirt at home? You're sure you can think of something.

And it's a success! You customise the knickerbockers and the shirt by throwing them in the bin, and sashay onstage in just your bra and Brazilian-cut knickers. All eyes are on you, and Carly throws you the dirtiest looks imaginable.

The only downside to your performance is that something's happened to the backing track – it's all out of key! You're singing all the right notes, but they don't match the music. Some idiot on the mixing desk has messed up, and when you find out who, they're going to pay.

The audience don't seem to mind too much, though. One teenage boy in particular, who's in the front row surrounded by a bunch of tough-looking guys with buzz cuts, can't seem to stop staring at you; he looks vaguely familiar.

'OMG, Shampayne, did you see Dustin Shelves in the audience?' Hollie shrieks excitedly as you come offstage. 'He couldn't take his eyes off you!'

Wow, is that who it was? Dustin Shelves is a teen sensation, one of the biggest pop stars in the world. And apparently, he was looking at you!

Within the hour there's a message from Dustin's agent on your mobile.

'Dustin told me 2 tell you he thinks u r fit,' you read aloud. Carly shoots you a murderous look. 'Will you go out with him?'

You're really flattered. Dustin's just seventeen, but already he's dated half the models, actresses and It Girls in LA and London. But you've heard he's trouble – he's been in rehab a few times, and his behaviour can be unstable, to say the least. Do you really need the hassle while your career is taking off?

If you want to go on a date with Dustin, go to 35 on page 152
If you'd rather concentrate on your career, go to 49 on page 206

27

Your belly looks like a Space Hopper, but it turns out there's a good reason – you're having *five babies*! Apparently, you and Reece are both super-fertile, and against all the odds, five of his sperm managed to find their way to the target.

'We find fertility is often inversely proportional to the size of the intellect,' explains the consultant obstetrician when you go for your first scan.

Reece is thrilled. 'Wow, I'm going to be a dad!' he says excitedly, looking at the screen. 'Look at that one's little face! He's *soo* cute!'

The consultant sighs. 'That's not the ultrasound you're looking at, Mr Sullivan, it's my iPhone,' he says wearily. 'I've used my five-year-old's drawing of SpongeBob SquarePants as a screensaver.'

You can barely concentrate on a word anyone's saying. *Five* babies? Just how fat are you going to get? And how will you cope?

'I'm going to be just like that Octomum in the States,' you wail.

Wannabe

'Not quite – that poor woman had *eight* babies,' says the consultant. 'Your babies are quins.'

Well, there's no need to be rude! But right now you're too concerned to take the consultant to task. Frankly, you're terrified. Your biggest fear is that your babies will have big noses or jug ears or something like that, but to your relief, the scan doesn't pick up any unattractive facial features. Which means you can concentrate on your second fear: how you'll cope financially. Channel 6 is going to film a new reality show when the babies finally arrive, but will that be enough?

It turns out your worries are groundless, as you manage to arrange for each of your babies to be sponsored by a different company. So when little Persil, Milton, Huggies, Dettol and Weetabix arrive in early spring, you're actually rolling in cash. To top it all, your babies are perfect – all of them have all their fingers and toes, and there are no ginger ones.

Of course, *Ooh La La!* has purchased exclusive rights to the first photoshoot.

'Shampayne, how are you finding motherhood?' the reporter asks.

'Hard work!' you smile. 'Especially all the crying and wailing!'

'I'm sorry, I shouldn't do that, really,' Reece chips in. 'It just gets a bit much sometimes, changing five babies' nappies and giving five babies their bottles. I get a bit tired, and sometimes I cry.'

The reporter turns to Reece. 'So do you wish Shampayne would do some of the hands-on stuff, Reece?'

'Oh, Reece knows I'm too busy,' you say.

'That's right,' Reece agrees. 'I don't want to interrupt Shampayne when she's watching daytime TV, or having a pedicure.'

'I do take them out and about, though,' you add. 'The other day I took them to a nature reserve, didn't I?'

Reece smiles. 'She did. When she went back to collect them at teatime there was a family of foxes playing with them.'

'There was one sitting right on Huggies' face, can you believe it? It was adorable! I took some lovely pictures.'

The reporter clears her throat. 'And what are your hopes and dreams for your children, Shampayne?'

'Well...' You think for a moment. 'The same as every mum, I suppose. I just want them to be famous.'

This is more than you've ever wanted: a husband – albeit a thick one – a brood of kids, and cameras in your house 24/7. You could do without a belly that looks like a deflated airbed, but a little nip and tuck will take care of that. Yes, readers, there's more to come from Shampayne Sullivan. But for now...

YOUR CELEBRITY ADVENTURE IS OVER

28

'I've got a great idea!', you tell your fellow glamour models, Stacey B and Abi D, as you're hanging around between shots.

'Really?' says Stacey, surprised. 'What is it?'

'I'm going to have a drink of water!'

You've just realised you're really thirsty. And when you're thirsty, that means your body needs fluids. And the teachers said you didn't listen at school... But just as you're rooting around in your bag for your Evian, you have *another* great idea – that's two in one day!

'Hey, you two,' you say, 'how about we form a girlband, and audition for *Star Quality*?'

Now Stacey and Abi are excited. This idea is *much* better than your water one!

'Yeah! That would be awesome!' trills Abi.

'Ooh, what shall we call ourselves?' asks Stacey.

You all think long and hard.

'How about The Three Bares?' suggests Abi.

'Nah, bit naff,' Stacey says.

You all think long and hard.

'I know!' you say. 'The Threesome!'

Abi frowns. 'I don't know, I'm not sure it sends the right message.'

You all think long and hard. My God, it's exhausting!

'Why don't we just stick our finger in a book, and we'll use the first words we land on?' Abi suggests. 'I named all my kids that way.'

You and Stacey laugh.

'As if! I mean, where are we gonna get a *book*?' you sneer.

'Aha!' Abi bends down and rummages in her bag. 'Look!' she says triumphantly, pulling out a copy of her diary. 'This will do, won't it?'

'It's a book, I suppose,' agrees Stacey.

'Close your eyes, then!' you say, as Abi flips through the pages with a perfectly manicured hand. 'Pick the first couple of words you point to!'

So that's how the Pregnancy Tests are formed.

You're a bit like Girls Aloud, in that you're all girls. And a bit like the Spice Girls in that at least one of you has given a Premiership footballer a blowjob. But in terms of talent and vocal style, people say you're like nothing they've ever heard before.

You bring Nana Rose along to hear you rehearse, and she's so moved that she has to leave the room.

Deciding what to sing at your audition gives the three of you another headache. You all have very different music tastes and each of you is keen to showcase what you can do vocally so in the end you decide on 'Knock Me Up Before You Go-Go', a mash-up of your favourite Wham! song and Amii Stewart's 'Knock On Wood'.

You rehearse non-stop, and all the hard work starts to pay off. You've worked out some slick dance moves, and picked out some brilliant costumes; you're all going to be wearing different styles of dresses. It's a great gimmick – Stacey will be in a tea dress because she loves tea, you'll be in a fishtail frock because you love fish, and Abi will be wearing a cocktail frock because she loves to dress up.

Finally, the day of the audition arrives. You've never felt more nervous – this could be your one and only chance to get into the music industry!

'Don't blow it, girls,' you whisper to Stacey and Abi as you wait backstage. 'We've only got one shot at this.'

You're most worried about head judge Damon Bowells, who is famous for dishing out harsh criticism. You can hear him right now, telling a seven-year-old girl her rendition of 'Edelweiss' was 'complete and utter crap', while ripping the arms and legs off her favourite teddy and force-feeding them to her kitten.

OMG, if you don't smash it, what's he going to do to you?

'Come on, Shampayne,' you tell yourself. 'Tits out, head up! Or is it head out, tits up?' You can't remember! As it turns out, it doesn't really matter. Damon seems delighted to see the three of you as you sashay on stage.

'It's a definite "yes" from me!' he quips, as Abi bends to adjust the hem of her dress, revealing her 38GG cleavage.

You manage one verse of your song before Damon cuts you off.

'Seriously, I like you girls,' he says. 'You're young, you're fresh. You're relevant.'

'We are!' you say keenly. 'We're really, *really* vant.'

You've no idea what he's talking about but you'll say whatever he wants to hear.

'You girls get my vote,' he says with wink. 'I want to see you at bootcamp.'

So it's a shock when the other judges – some well jel old hag and some guy who looks like a garden gnome – vote no.

'It's a travesty!' yells Damon, looking furious. 'These girls have got something really special!'

'Damon, they can't sing!' protests the garden gnome.

'We just don't feel any chemistry between them,' says the hag.

What if that one comes back without the others, as a solo artist?' Damon suggests, pointing at you. 'What do you think, sweetheart, want to try again on your own?'

Stacey and Abi put their arms around you protectively.

'We're a team,' Stacey says defiantly. 'You can't split us up.'

'This is *so hard* for me,' you say tearfully. 'These girls are like family to me. I can't abandon them.'

Damon shrugs. 'Okay, it's your loss.'

'Oh, alright then,' you say, shrugging off Stacey and Abi's hands. 'I'll do "Chasing Pavements" by Adele.'

'Bitch!' whispers Abi.

Bit harsh, you think. What's Adele ever done to her?

The other Pregnancy Tests are ushered offstage, and you stand alone in the spotlight. The audience have been murmuring, debating your decision, but now they fall silent: they're waiting for you to begin.

The first chords drift across from the wings. You count yourself in... two, three, four...

'I've...' you sing.

Wannabe

Damon holds up a hand. 'Wait,' he says. 'I've changed my mind. Bring back the one with the bigger knockers!'

And that was the exact moment, you realise later, when you decided you need a boob job. Even though your 30EEs are pretty impressive, especially when attached to your teeny-weeny frame, you keep missing out on opportunities to curvier girls. It's starting to get you down. But what size should you go?

If you want to enlarge your breasts to 30G, go to 39 on page 162
If you want to go up to 30JJ, go to 20 on page 88

29

The reviews for *Laydeez* are fantastic!

'Shampayne Sullivan excels as the vapid and thoroughly dislikeable Jemima,' *Entertainment Now* enthuses. 'Her dead-eyed stare and flat delivery expertly convey the gaping void where the character's soul should be.'

'At turns irritating and pitiable,' trumpets *Showbiz* magazine.

'Like a blow-up doll sleepwalking her way through each episode,' announces the *New York Recorder*.

This is amazing! Better than you could have hoped. There could definitely be a Golden Globe in it for you.

You're *so hot* right now. You brush past an old lady in the shops and she bursts into flames. Hobos gather round your house at night, warming their hands on your hotness. The Fire Department warn you not to go hiking in the forest, at least not without a portable fire extinguisher. You're loving all the attention, and people are saying such great things about you. Channel-surfing, you come across an Alana Durban interview; she's gushing about your performance. 'Shampayne is an *incredible* method actor,' she enthuses. 'She stayed in character the whole time when the cameras weren't running. In fact, if you talk to her, you'll find she's *still* in character now. That's how dedicated she is to her art.'

There's only one thing missing from your life: someone to share it with. You should be part of a power couple. You need someone to complete you, to raise your profile. Like Brangelina, or Kimye, or Bey-Jay. What would go nicely with Shampayne?

You find out soon enough, when you first set eyes on C-Rock.

You're lunching with your new agent, Sheryl Bitchenberger, at Chi Spacca on Melrose Avenue, discussing whether or not butt implants would help your career. You've just ordered a Salade Niçoise, LA-style – minus the eggs, the tuna, the olives, the new potatoes, the tomatoes, the dressing, and the green beans – and an H2O-free sparkling water, when across the restaurant you spot a gorgeous, muscular black guy in head-to-toe leather and mirrored shades.

'That guy over there, he looks familiar. Who is he?' you ask.

Sheryl glances over. 'Don't you *know*?' She's incredulous. 'That's C-Rock. I guess he must be in town for the Grammys – he's up for five this year.'

You toy with your lettuce leaves. 'Is he single?'

'As far as I know,' says Sheryl. 'Do you want me to get my people to make contact with his people, and ask if he'd like to go on a high-profile, public date with you? Maybe an LA Lakers game, or a fashion show?'

'That's okay,' you say, 'I'll take care of it myself.'

'That's not how we do things in LA!' Sheryl calls after you as you snake your way across the restaurant.

Wannabe

Maybe not, but slithering on your belly and hissing is guaranteed to get C-Rock's attention.

You slither to a stop at C-Rock's feet. 'Hi,' you say, coiling your body around his leg. 'Care to buy me a drink?'

C-Rock looks shocked. Two of his entourage stand up and move towards you threateningly, but he waves them away. 'It's okay,' he says, 'I think she's just British.'

You uncoil yourself from C-Rock's leg and slither your way onto his lap. 'That's right,' you purr, mixing your animal metaphors shamelessly, 'you might know me from *Laydeez*. I'm Shampayne Sullivan.'

'Hey, I thought I recognised you!' C-Rock is smiling now. 'It's okay, guys, she's cool.'

C-Rock's entourage visibly relax. So you're not just not some random crazed madwoman, you're a *celebrity* crazed madwoman.

C-Rock is meanwhile looking you up and down, as if he'd like to gobble you up. He really is gorgeous, close-up. He's just the way you like your men: skin like chocolate, big, soulful eyes, and a full set of gold grillz.

You flick back a strand of your hair seductively. It lands in someone's soup on the opposite side of the restaurant – you really shouldn't have had those cut-price extensions. Luckily, C-Rock doesn't seem to have noticed. He's gazing deep into your eyes.

'I ain't trippin' when I tell you, girl,' he says softly,

'You got ma mind and body in a whirl

You got the style, you got the attitude

I wanna grab ya and do something rude...'

It's as if time is standing still. All you can see and hear is C-Rock. You think you could really be falling for this guy.

Wannabe

'Why don't you come on over to my crib?

Forget about your women's lib

First thing I'll do is strip you bare

Give it to you on the rocking chair...'

You open your mouth to speak...

'Don't say no, girl, that'd make me sad

You're the hottest thing I never had

Tweet me later when you're all alone

Or send a selfie to me on your phone.

I'm gonna dream about your face tonight

Picture you in something nice and tight

Say you will, girl, say you'll be my boo...'

Okay, so it's getting a little bit annoying now. You can't get a word in edgeways.

You put your finger gently on C-Rock's lips. 'Right now I'm bustin' for the loo,' you murmur,

'But ring my agent if you want a date

Meeting you feels right, I think it's fate

I'm usually free Monday through to Thursday but not this Friday coming, or at the weekend because I have Ashtanga Yoga Boot Camp.'

Okay, that last bit went slightly wrong but you're pretty sure you've made the right impression. You sashay to the ladies' toilets, wiggling your butt seductively and glancing back over your shoulder to where C-Rock is sitting, a string of drool emerging from one corner of his mouth.

You're on a high – C-Rock has asked you out! This could be a match made in corporate heaven. Just think what you could achieve as a team; you'd attract the biggest brands – Patek Philippe, Tiffany, Ralph Lauren... There's huge potential in hooking up. If you can just put up with C-Rock rapping everything, you could really go places.

At first, C-Rock seems like the perfect A-list boyfriend. But it soon becomes clear that his ego is out of control. His entourage, for starters, is the biggest you've ever seen. He has a manager, a deputy manager and an assistant manager; six security personnel, three chauffeurs, a personal stylist and an emergency personal stylist; a flunkey, a flunkey's assistant and a junior flunkey; a fixer, a backscratcher, two lackeys and a fluffer – an attractive brunette whose job, according to C-Rock, is to pick fluff out of his belly button.

For a first date, C-Rock gets one of his chauffeurs to drive you out to his hacienda in the Hollywood Hills. He's waiting on the front steps for you as you pull up. 'Welcome to C-Rock's crib,' he says as his Official Door-Handle Turner turns the handle of the front door, and his Chief Door Opener pushes it open.

You step inside. C-Rock follows behind; he's being given a piggyback by his Personal Threshold Crossing Enabler. You're stunned by what you see. With its acres of marble, gold leaf and glittering chandeliers, the interior would remind you of the Palace of Versailles, if only you had a clue what that was. But seeing as you don't, you just dribble a bit and say, 'Oooh, pretty!'

'Check out the faux-Rococo stucco work,' says C-Rock.

'It's enough to make your booty twerk.

Paid $60 thousand for my marble floors

Got gold-leaf panelling on all my doors…'

He takes your hand and you follow him across the hallway, towards a vast, sweeping staircase that leads up to the first floor.

'But now's not the time to talk décor

Wannabe

Girl, remember what you came here for,

C-Rock is gonna rock your body

Afterwards you'll...' – he pauses for a minute, frowning – '... need a hot toddy.'

And it's true – you do. If only to get over the disappointment.

You should have guessed C-Rock might have 'niche interests' the minute you set eyes on his bedroom.

'Take no notice of my cuddly toys,' he'd whispered in your ear as he pulled you close.

'They ain't bothered if we make a noise

They know just what you came here for

My Little Pony's seen it all before.'

You pull C-Rock towards the bed. Reaching behind you, you sweep a few of the teddies and other toys off the embroidered eiderdown and onto the floor. C-Rock immediately bends down and picks them up.

'Watch out, girl, they're my prized possessions

They've witnessed all my bonking sessions...'

He waves a fluffy blue bunny in your face.

'I love this rabbit here just like a brother

This doll reminds me of my mother...'

You kiss him, just to shut him up. 'Oh, C-Rock,' you murmur, as you come up for air. 'I want you, and your marketing potential, so badly!'

You kiss him again before he has a chance to reply, and pretty soon rapping is the last thing on C-Rock's mind. You're finding it hard to relax, though. Usually you're game for anything but you find being watched by stuffed animals while you're having sex surprisingly inhibiting. You can see Winnie the Pooh staring at you with beady eyes, and there's a Furby uncomfortably close to *your* furby. C-Rock, on the other hand, seems to find it a turn-on. At the point of no return, he reached out and fondled the Furby's beak, which, to be honest, made you feel a bit of a spare part.

Afterwards, C-Rock collapses back onto the bed, with you nestled under one arm and Elmer the Patchwork Elephant under the other. You're not sure what to make of it all. It seems kind of weird, but maybe it's just how people are in LA?.

Should you stick around, and see where your relationship with C-Rock takes you? Or leave him to his furry friends and get the hell out?

If you want to stick with C-Rock, go to 40 on page 166
If you'd rather be single, go to 8 on page 33

30

You and Dean are finished! You can hardly believe it – your first real boyfriend, the first man (with a van) to make love to you, and it's over.

Back at home, you throw yourself onto the sofa and weep bitter tears. Who will take you for your weekly bikini wax now? 'Oh, Swimmy,' you wail, 'how will I find the strength to go on?' Poor Swimmy can't bear to see you like this, and disappears into his little pineapple house. He's the only one who understands you.

You spend the week leading up to the competition working on your vocals. Nana Rose helps you with the costume. You were thinking of a little vest-and-pants ensemble like Miley Cyrus wore in her *Wrecking Ball* video, but Nana Rose persuades you that a floaty white dress would look 'more demure'. Personally, you don't want to look like Demi Moore – she's *ancient*, for God's sake – but you don't want to risk arguing with Nana Rose when she's holding a pair of scissors, so you let her run something up from a pair of old net curtains.

Wannabe

You have to admit, though, she knows best. In your new white lace number you look innocent and virginal… if you squint a bit. Nana Rose has tears in her eyes when you give her a twirl. 'Oh, love,' she sighs, 'you look like Kate Middleclass on her wedding day – if she'd had two beach balls up her dress!'

'Do you think the judges will like it?' you ask hopefully.

'Of course they will. And if they don't, I'll set Satan on them!'

You've got butterflies in your tummy as you head through the lounge bar to where the other contestants are gathering, so it's a relief when you spot a few people you know. A couple of girls from your school's cheerleading squad are there, fiddling nervously with their pompoms. Another boy from school, Spencer something – who you're pretty sure fancies you – is also waiting for his turn. His eyes nearly pop out of his head when he sees you standing there in your tight white dress. He'll be stiff competition.

'Shampayne Sullivan, you're next!' One of the bar staff ushers you towards the makeshift stage at the back of the pub.

You're up!

'Good luck!' Spencer mouths.

Fighting down waves of nausea you make your way onto the stage. There are lights shining in your eyes and you can't see the audience, but you know Nana Rose and Satan are out there somewhere, willing you to do well.

A hush falls over the pub. You give a quick nod towards the wings, and the first notes of 'Ave Maria' float through the air. Then the bassline kicks in, and the snare drum – you're glad you did that remix, the churchy version is *sooooo* dull – and you start to gyrate to the music, breathing out the lyrics as seductively as you can. You soon realise you can't remember all the exact words, but you figure it won't matter; no one else will know them either, as they're all in Italianish anyway.

'Ave Maria, Maria, Maria,' you breathe. 'I'm a survivor, I'm gonna make it, I will survive, Keep on survivin'...' Ooh, it's turning into a mash-up!

The pub regulars have clearly never heard anything like it; you can just make out an elderly couple near the front, staring up at you, open-mouthed. You've smashed it!

You come to the end of the song, and decide to round things off by doing the splits.

'Well done, love!' Nana Rose's voice rings out. 'She was bloody brilliant, wasn't she?'

The audience are silent – it's as if they're in a trance.

'I *said*,' – Nana sounds more menacing this time – 'she was brilliant, *wasn't* she?'

There's a ripple of applause, and a low murmur runs around the pub.

You take a quick bow and run offstage – straight into Spencer. 'That was, um... really original,' he mumbles. He knows he's got no chance now. Too bad, there can only be one winner. Global superstardom, here you come...

'You were robbed, love,' Nana Rose says, squeezing your shoulders consolingly. 'They don't know what talent is.'

She's right – you were clearly the best by miles.

You're sobbing your heart out, your mascara making streaky patterns all down the front of your white dress. How *could* you have come last?

'Maybe they weren't ready for you,' Spencer suggests. 'It was a little bit... *avant garde*.'

Wannabe

You're starting to think Spencer might be gay.

You dab at your eyes with your sleeve. 'It was maybe too modern,' you sniff. 'The Countryside is a very old-fashioned place.'

'Well, I think they've made a *big* mistake,' Nana Rose says menacingly. 'I'll just go and have a word. Come on, Satan...'

And incredibly, it turns out Nana Rose is right! There *has* been a huge mistake, and that boy who could juggle fire while riding a unicycle and singing the Korean national anthem should have come last instead of first.

And there's an even bigger surprise waiting for you when you reach the car park – Dean! He's standing beside his van, carrying a huge bunch of red roses.

'Oh, babe,' you say, throwing yourself into his arms. 'I won! Are you pleased for me?'

'Yes, I am. I can't stay mad at you,' he admits. 'I tried shagging Louise, and Emma, then Shelley, for old times' sake, but it just didn't feel the same. Come on...' He opens the van door for you. 'I'll take you home.'

You clamber in. You can tell Dean's made an effort for you – the van smells of pine disinfectant, and he's pushed all the used tissues into a neat little pile. You're touched.

'I've missed you,' he murmurs, burying his face in your hair extensions.

Just then, there's a tap on the window. Dean winds it down.

'Yes, mate?'

A man with a stubbly chin and sunglasses perched on top of his head leans in. Quite what a stubbly chin is doing on his head is anyone's guess. You can only suppose he's not from around these parts.

'I'm a talent agent,' he says in a husky voice, holding out a business card. 'I'd like you to call me, Shampayne.'

'Oh!' you say. 'Shampayne's my name, too!'

What a coincidence!

The man looks pained. '*No*, my name's Vince Vole,' he says slowly. 'I'd like *you*, *Shampayne*, to give *me* a ring.'

You take the card and look at it.

'Martin Cross, Probation Officer, Countryshire Sexual Offenders Treatment Programme' you read.

'Nah, wrong one,' says Vince, snatching the card back. He takes another from the waistcoat of his three-piece suit.

'Vincent Vole, Vole Variety,' you read. Well, it certainly looks professional. This could be it, the big time!

'I see something in you, Shampayne,' Vince says, his dark eyes piercing yours. 'You've got something special.'

'Right, thanks, mate,' says Dean briskly, bringing you back to reality. His hands are gripping the steering wheel tightly. You hope he's not going to fly into one of his jealous rages. 'We've got to be off,' he says, putting the van into first and revving the engine.

'Sure, sure...' Vince takes a step back and hooks his thumbs into the belt loops of his suit, and leans back on the heels of his cowboy boots. He looks like Robin Thicke's older, plumper, shorter, less attractive brother, you think to yourself as the van pulls out of the car park.

'I don't like the look of him,' Dean mutters as he slams the van into second gear.

'Well, I thought he seemed nice,' you say.

Is Dean going back to his old ways already? You hoped he was going to support you, not give you a hard time.

'Listen, Shampayne, I've been thinking...' he says.

Wannabe

That doesn't sound like Dean.

His face looks pained – thinking obviously takes it out of him. 'Shampayne Sullivan,' he says in a serious voice, 'will you marry me?'

WTF?

'I mean it, let's tie the knot. I want to be with you forever.'

Wow, this is like something out of *The Notebook*! You're over-whelmed.

'Oh, Dean,' you sigh. 'It's such a surprise! I don't know what to say!'

'Say yes, Shampayne. You know how good we are together.'

It's true. No one else comes close. Wouldn't it be a dream come true to marry Dean and be the mother of his third batch of children? But this is a big decision. It looks like your showbiz career could finally be taking off. If you marry Dean, you know he won't be happy about you working with Vince...

OMG, what are you going to do?

If you want to finish with Dean and ring Vince, go to 18 on page 79

If you want to marry Dean, go to 4 on page 17

31

It's the morning of your first glamour shoot. You've spent the past week buffing and polishing yourself into tip-top shape, and although you know you look as good as you possibly can, you're still nervous.

There are so many people in the studio – not just the photographer, but a bearded guy fiddling with the lighting, a couple of make-up girls, a motorcycle courier who's dropping off a package and a random traffic warden who's wandered in off the street. Are you really going to have to get naked in front of them all?

'Be brave, Shampayne!' you whisper to yourself. 'This is your time to shine!'

'Shammi! So nice to meet you!' Linda Lovely, the photographer, is making her way across the studio towards you. A legend in the glamour business, she used be a Page 3 Girl, way back in the 1980s, and what she doesn't know about making mammary glands look good isn't worth knowing.

'Don't be nervous, darling, you're in safe hands!' Linda says, sensing your apprehension. She sizes you up. 'Hmmm, you're taller than I'd thought. Great legs, good arse!'

A twentysomething Asian guy with purple hair appears at her side. Linda introduces you.

'Shampayne, this is Cho, he'll get you camera-ready.'

Cho looks at you with distaste.

'Did you wax?' he asks, holding up a pair of tweezers. 'Or do we need to tidy up the garden?'

'It's not a garden, it's a patio,' you say confidently. 'And I had it power-washed yesterday.'

You're glad you let Olga at Spartan Spa persuade you to have that Vaginal Sandblast treatment now.

Cho looks relieved.

'Thong, or tanga?'

He waves towards a Perspex box at the side of the room. It's filled with flimsy items of underwear.

'Slutty workout gear,' you say confidently. 'Legwarmers and satin hotpants.'

That's it, Shampayne, you tell yourself, you're the one in control. You know the look you're after.

Cho raises his expertly threaded eyebrows. 'Interesting – I'd have said French knickers and lacy gloves,' he says, looking thoughtful. 'But we'll try it your way.'

And it turns out you're a natural in front of the camera. It's hardly a surprise – you've been practising for years, in front of the mirror at home, in the school toilets, in car windscreens, ponds and rivers… Anywhere there's a reflective surface. And you've done your research on the main glamour poses, so you know you can pull off the Hand-Bra (hands holding up your breasts), the

Wannabe

Sexy Earthworm (lying on your front, but lifting your butt towards the ceiling), the Help, I've Fallen Over Really Awkwardly (spread-eagled on the ground with your legs up against a wall), and the Aftermath of a Tornado in Claire's Accessories (naked apart from a pair of deely-boppers and a plastic day-glo necklace). Of course, there's also the Look What I Had For Supper! (legs akimbo), but you're not planning on going there yet.

'That's brilliant, Shampayne,' Linda calls as she clicks away. 'It's like you were born to do this.'

You turn your body into some interesting poses, and some surprising new ones that Linda's never seen before.

'How do you *do* that?' she asks, as you twist your torso 180 degrees so your boobs and buttocks are facing the camera at the same time.

'Just supple, I guess.'

All too soon the shoot is over. You don't want it to end, you've enjoyed yourself so much. Linda shows you the results on her laptop. You can hardly believe it's you – you look so grown-up and sexy.

'These are fantastic,' Linda enthuses. 'You're gonna be huge, babe!'

'Yeah, I can see that,' says a husky voice behind you. 'I can imagine she'll be huge *all over* some day. Probably after she's had a baby.'

You turn around to see who's spoken, and to your surprise it isn't a husky at all – it's Lacey Lamberton, the UK's leading glamour model and cow. Your first impression is one of bouncy chestnut curls, big green eyes and huge brown boobs. There's no denying she's a stunning woman.

'Lacey, darling!' Linda and Lacey air-kiss.

'I've just popped in to talk about tomorrow's shoot,' Lacey drawls. 'But I can see you've got your work cut out here.'

'No, we're just about done,' Linda smiles. 'Come on through to the office. Thanks, Shampayne, you can put your clothes back on now.'

Lacey flashes you a fake smile. 'I'd say "See you around", but I probably won't.'

You feel your blood starting to boil. It takes a lot to get you angry, but when your temper's unleashed, everyone had better get the hell out of your way. At secondary school your nickname was Nut Job, and you don't think people were referring to the fact that you worked at the macadamia processing plant on Saturdays. Well, now you actually think about it, maybe they were...

Whatever, part of you wants to follow Lacey, grab her by her fake hair, wrestle her to the ground, slap her around the trout pout a few times, and pull off her false eyelashes. And possibly force her to eat them, too – it depends how psychotic you're feeling. The other half of you is holding back. Attacking the UK's leading glamour model and cow wouldn't do your career much good. Linda would probably never allow you near her studio again. But boy, would it feel good to pummel Lacey Lamberton into the ground...

What should you do?

If you want to slap Lacey's smug face, go to 21 on page 93
If you'd rather backstab her at a later date, go to 28 on page 122

32

Antonio and Angela are the first to be voted out after they fail the 'Eat each other's dirty socks' task. The public must like you, though, as you're still here. Or maybe they're waiting for a catfight with Francesca. There's certainly a strange atmosphere when it's just the four of you left. Francesca doesn't make any attempt to talk to you. You don't get it – she's a total bitch, you're a total bitch. In any other universe you'd be friends.

You discover just how huge a bitch Francesca is on day 21, when you're coming out of the Bitch Box. You'd gone in there for a good old moan about Lizzard never emptying the dishwasher, and quite honestly you feel better for it. But wait a minute – *what the hell's going on?* Randy is lying flat on his back on one of the conversation couches and Francesca – wearing just a teensy string bikini – is straddling him.

You march over. 'What do you think you're doing?'

Francesca flicks her long blonde hair over her shoulder. 'Randy

Wannabe

is just opening up my chakras,' she says, with a smug smile. Neither of them attempts to move. 'Ooooh,' Randy is chanting. 'Eeeee.... Aaaaaah... Zzzzz....'

'Yes, but why do you have to sit on him like that?' you snap.

Randy stops chanting. 'She's connecting with my third eye,' he says. 'Zzzzz... Eeeeee... Aaaaaaah...'

Francesca gives a little gasp of surprise. 'Oh, I think your root chakra is activated now!'

That's it – you've had it with Randy! You thought he was different, but now you realise he's just like every other man you've known. He's made you look a fool in front of millions of viewers... when you were quite capable of doing that all on your own.

Calmly, you walk over to the kitchen area and grab the bin; it's full to the brim with vegetable peelings and leftover pasta. 'I am an overflowing cup of love!' you chant, as you pour the contents over Randy and Francesca's heads. 'The universe expresses itself through me, fuckers, for I am a beacon of shining light!'

As a result of that you come out of *Buffoon Bungalow* pretty well. You've dropped five places on the Most Hated Celebrity poll in *Chitchat* magazine. The media are on your side, too. 'It's a SHAM DUNK!' the *Daily Maul* announces, alongside a picture of Randy wearing an upturned Brabantia.

This is your moment! If you play your cards right, this could translate into something big. But what?

If you want to write your autobiography, go to 38 on page 160
If you want to get into TV presenting, go to 37 on page 157

33

As you get closer, you see it's not Bobbie Dicke at all – just a sleazy-looking estate agent in a shiny suit, Cuban heels and mirrored shades.

Oh well, easy mistake to make.

You brush past each other, and as you do, a familiar scent hits you: QuidChem's 'Man Juice'. You'd recognise it anywhere – it was Dean's favourite aftershave.

A wave of sadness washes over you. You're all alone in the showbusiness ocean, adrift without a boyfriend for company. Fighting back tears, you think about what Dean and Kyle both used to give you: lifts. If things had been different either one of them would be here, now, waiting outside in the rain to take you home. As it is, you'll have to get the Tube, or, God help you, a bus.

The words of Boylove's 1992 smash, 'I'll Be There, Baby', flood into your head:

'When you need a lift, I will be there

Wannabe

If you need 20 quid, I'll sub you, Baby
Need some sanitary towels from the corner shop?
I'll take care of that for you, 'cos you're my lady.'

That's real love, you think, dabbing your eyes with a tissue. Something that's lacking in your life right now. Of course, you still have Swimmy. And there's Nana Rose and Satan but it's not the same: none of them can drive.

Dean and Kyle would have done anything for you, but there's no going back, the past is the past. What you need is to find someone new, someone who'll cherish you, care for you and worship the ground you walk on. Someone who's not averse to waiting outside in any type of weather for four hours while you get your extensions done. You're not fussy – it could be a guy or a girl. You're not looking for intelligence, or even for amazing looks, but you *are* looking for a car!

If you want to find love with a guy, go to 12 on page 50
If you want to find love with a girl, go to 5 on page 18

34

There's only one thing to do: a workout DVD.

This means hooking up with personal trainer to the stars, Tony Thrust. The best in the business, he never divulges his client list but rumour has it that he's had a hand in the perfect butts of at least half Hollywood's best-known actresses.

'No shame, no gain' is his motto. His approach to fitness is unusual: he insists his clients exercise in public, in full view of the paparazzi, wearing unflattering skimpy gym gear that's clearly three sizes too small until they're humilated into losing weight. You can't wait to meet him in the flesh.

And he doesn't disappoint...

Tony Thrust is a man-mountain. You've arranged to meet him in the lobby of the Central London Hotel, and at first you mistake his huge, bronzed body for a walk-in wardrobe, and try to hang up your coat in him. He's just the way you like your men: pumped up and ripped, like a cheap air bed.

Wannabe

'Hi, Shampayne, it's great to meet you,' Tony says, crushing your hand with his powerful fingers. You feel your pinkie almost snap in half, but you don't care. He's staring into your eyes, hard, with the intensity of a boxer pummelling a punch bag. You have a funny feeling in the pit of your stomach.

'I need help with my muffin top,' you murmur, 'and I think you're the perfect guy to do it.'

His gaze carries on pummelling yours, your gaze collapses onto the ropes. For a moment you're locked in a staring competition: who's going to blink first? But just as suddenly the spell is broken.

'Excuse me a minute,' Tony says, and drops to the floor for 20 one-armed press ups. 'If I don't exercise every 1.5 minutes, my muscles will start to atrophy,' he pants. 'Right now, I'm targeting the pectorals, triceps, and shoulders, using the lower trapezius and the serratus anterior for stability, and engaging my core, too.'

Wow, he really knows his stuff! If anyone can help you tone up, it's this guy.

'Why don't you get down with me, and give me 10 burpees?' he suggests.

'What, right here? In the lobby?' (You're wearing 5-inch heels.)

'I need to see what you're made of!' he explains. 'Squat thrusts, go!'

Reluctantly, you crouch down on your haunches and give a half-hearted little bunny hop.

'Make it count, Shampayne!' he bellows. 'Feel the burn!'

You give another hop – already your calves are hurting.

Tony straightens up, and puts his foot on your shoulder. 'Now try it!' he barks.

Wannabe

You collapse on the marble floor. One heel of your shoe snaps off.

That means you've lost ½oz already! It's a great start.

Your DVD, *Sweat with Shampayne*, is a huge success. It features four 15-minute workouts: for the lower body, the chest, the abs, and the hair. And you're the best advert for it there can be: thanks to Tony's punishing workouts, you've lost 3lb. Your muffin top has disappeared, your legs and bum are toned and shapely, and your hair is the most supple and shiny it's been in years.

You've worked hard in the gym together but mostly, you and Tony have been working out in the sack. He's an incredible lover – so strong and powerful! He makes you feel like a fencepost being driven into the ground by a piledriver. Or like a chicken fillet being tenderised by a meat mallet. You really think you could be falling in love with this man.

There's only one problem. Well, there are several problems, actually:

1 He supports Norwich City.

2 His favourite band is The Script.

3 He calls his penis 'Mr Wiggles'.

4 You've seen a sump pump suck up floodwater more delicately than he slurps his soup.

But they're just minor niggles, really, compared to 'the big issue': namely, that his boobs are larger, and perkier, than yours. Everywhere you go as a couple, *he's* the one who turns heads. Especially when he insists on borrowing your bikini.

'I'm comfortable with my sexuality,' he tells you, squeezing his gigantic buttocks into your satin hotpants.

'But you're too big for my clothes, Tony,' you tell him,

wincing as you hear the fabric rip. 'You need to get some in a larger size.'

'I'm expressing my alter ego, Coco,' he protests, 'and she's a size zero.'

Things come to a head when you're holidaying in Dubai, and Tony/Coco gets three pap shots in the *Daily Maul*, while you only get one. 'Tony Thrust shows off his enviable bikini body,' you read. 'The personal trainer looked toned and curvaceous in a white Spandex two-piece as he hit the beach at the exclusive Habtoor Grand resort. His killer abs and pert pectorals stunned envious onlookers as he frolicked in the water with his girlfriend, Shampayne Sullivan, who also looked quite nice.'

What's more, his pictures are right at the top of the page, and yours is just a little itty-bitty extra on the bottom left. No one puts Shampayne in the corner! Tony's clearly going to have to go. But you don't regret your relationship: thanks to him, you're in the best shape you've ever been. So much so that you've had an exciting new offer: to model in the Brandi-Lynn's Dirty Panties show, one of the biggest Stateside annual underwear-related events.

It could be the start of a whole new adventure for you. Or you could just stay home – something will turn up, right?

If you want to try knicker modelling, go to 54 on page 222
If you want to stay home, go to 43 on page 176

35

At first Dustin seems like the perfect man-child. His energy is so infectious. When the two of you finally get to meet up, at an arcade near his record company's office, he jumps up and down with excitement.

'Wow! You're really, really pretty!' he gasps. He takes off his baseball cap and runs his hand through his heavily gelled hair. It sticks for a moment, but he manages to tug it out.

'Wanna get out of here?' he asks shyly, 'I know a cool park we can go to!'

When you hang back, he tugs at your jacket. 'Aw, c'mon, it'll be brilliant,' he pleads. 'They've got this *awesome* new climbing frame. We can get a Sherbet Dip Dab from the corner shop!'

He breaks into a run. 'Come on,' he calls over his shoulder. 'Race you!'

You have to admit, despite it being difficult to play chase in 4in wedges, it's great fun being with Dustin, he's so carefree.

'Wheeeeeee!' he shouts as he goes headfirst down the slide. 'Why don't you get on the roundabout? I'll push!'

'Wow, this is awesome,' he shrieks. 'Look, Shampayne, look! Look how high I can go on the swings!'

After your first date, things move pretty fast. Within days, you've moved into Dustin's hotel suite. But that's when you first realise he has issues. He stays up late reading *The Beano* by torchlight and then he's really grumpy the next day. He forgets to change his socks and pants unless you remind him to. And when his room-service tea's on the table you have to call him, like, 20 times before he comes.

But Dustin's real problem is the amount of sweets he eats.

That's not to say *you* never indulge. You love Liquorice Allsorts, and you never could resist a Fizzy Cola Bottle, but your sweet-eating is mostly social, and at weekends. If you're out and someone offers you a Pear Drop, say, you'll have one, maybe two. But you know when to stop.

Dustin doesn't seem to have any limits. He can eat more sweets in one sitting than anyone else you've ever known. And then there's the sugar rush to deal with. It's not much fun trying to calm him down as he goes zooming about the room pretending to be an aeroplane or machine-gunning imaginary aliens.

Weekends become all about getting hold of more sweets. On Saturdays when Dustin's record company gives him his £2 pocket money, he spends it all at the pick 'n' mix counter. And when the money's gone, he hangs about outside the newsagents, bumming penny chews off ten-year-olds.

One afternoon he comes home literally reeking of Polo mints. There's sherbet all down his denim jacket, too.

'Dustin, this has *got* to stop,' you plead with him. 'If nothing else, think of your teeth!'

Wannabe

'Get off my case!' he protests. 'You're acting like my mom or something. It's getting really boring.'

God, maybe he's right? Maybe you *are* boring? Perhaps, if you don't stop being so uptight all the time, he'll find another girl he can enjoy Hubba Bubba with?

'C'mon, baby, relax a bit,' he cajoles. He rifles in his pocket. 'Here, have a white-chocolate mouse.'

Wow, it does look good! You shouldn't, really. But you can't afford to put on weight in your line of work. One little mouse can't hurt, can it?

If you eat the mouse, go to 51 on page 212
If you resist, go to 52 on page 215

36

Lee keeps snakes. He has literally hundreds of them, housed in cages and glass tanks arranged about his garage. The room smells acrid, and is uncomfortably hot; your make-up is sliding down your face. 'Sorry, I need to keep the temperature at tropical levels,' Lee explains, adjusting the thermostat, 'otherwise the snakes get poorly.'

He removes a cloth from a small cage at ground level. 'This one's fascinating,' he says, indicating a tiny bluish-black snake draped over a log. 'It's a Common Indian Krait. Can you see, there, that its scales are hexagonal and distinctly enlarged?' You nod politely. 'These snakes have pronounced dorsolateral flattening,' Lee continues. 'They're triangular in cross section and they commonly grow to around a metre in length, but specimens as large as 1.75m have been observed in the wild.' You check your watch. 'Kraits are ophiophagous, preying primarily upon other snakes, although they will eat mice and small lizards.'

Wannabe

'Wow,' you say. 'You sure love snakes.' This night isn't turning out quite the way you hoped it would.

'Now, are you ready to see my prize python?' he asks with a twinkle in his eye. Before you can reply he's taken you by the hand and is leading you to the darkest corner of the room. There's a ping! and then a groan as a cage door swings open.

OMG! Lee's python is *huge!* You've never seen one like it!

'You can touch it if you like,' Lee says encouragingly.

'Maybe later,' you reply politely. There's something about the python's clammy-looking skin that turns your stomach.

'What's *your* favourite snake?' Lee asks.

At last! You thought he'd never ask.

'The trouser snake,' you breathe sexily, twining your arms around his body. 'Why don't you show me yours?'

Lee's face falls. 'But I haven't showed you my boomslang yet!'

Bloody hell! All this guy cares about is snakes! You realise you're wasting your time... and wasting the reader's time, too. All this effort, and 450 or so words, just for the sake of one puerile joke likening penises to snakes. It's time to get out of here...

If you want to hear more about snakes, buy a book on them
If you want to see what happens next, go to 42 on page 172

37

'And now for *Newsnight*, with Kirsty Wark and Shampayne Sullivan...'

No, you're not sure how it happened either.

The only thing you know about politics is that it's really, really boring, and now you've been poached to co-present the BBC's flagship current-affairs programme.

'We're trying to attract a new demographic to *Newsnight*,' the producers explain. 'Our audience is mostly middle-aged, middle class and university educated. We need to attract more sixteen-to twenty-five-year-old males, and prisoners. You're just what we need to sex *Newsnight* up a bit!'

But the press don't seem too happy about your appointment. Especially when you ask George Osborne how his brother Ozzy is. And when you tweet about 'former French President Nicolas Teacosy'. But they were easy mistakes to make, and you're learning all the time. You're determined to prove all the haters wrong.

Wannabe

There's another, unexpected upturn in your life, too: you've met someone special.

You're not allowed to reveal his name, even in the pages of your own autobiography, but your nickname for him is 'Mr Pres'.

You met him when you interviewed him for a *Newsnight Special* on America's welfare reforms, and you were attracted to him right away. He's the most powerful, masterful, internationally famous man you've ever met.

'What's your favourite ice cream flavour?' you asked him, trying not to lose yourself in his deep brown eyes.

'Now, that's an interesting question...' He smiled and you felt a fluttering sensation in the pit of your stomach. 'It's not one I'm often asked. Um, I guess, I like any of the fruity ones.'

'Can you be more specific?' Your *Newsnight* bosses had told you to be tough on him. 'I need you to pick just one.'

'Strawberry, then.'

'That's my favourite, too!' you gush. 'And my second favourite is Raspberry Ripple!'

Mr Pres nods. 'That's a great flavour.'

Wow – it's like you're soulmates or something! It's clear you were meant to be together, and you're sure he thinks so too. You're equally sure his wife and kids don't, but what do they know?

You managed to struggle through the rest of the interview – you're a professional journalist now, after all – and find out Mr Pres's favourite film, the one thing he'd take to a desert island, and his Most Embarrasing Moment, even though it felt as if your heart was going to beat out of your chest.

You've never felt this way before about any celebrity.

But getting close to Mr Pres is tough. He's always surrounded by security people and hangers-on; his job is hugely demanding, almost as demanding as yours.

'I can't be with you as often as I'd like, Shampayne,' he tells you sadly, brushing away your tears. 'It's time-consuming being the P******** of the U***** S***** of A******.'

You sigh and press up against him. 'One day, when your divorce comes through, we'll be together forever, won't we?'

Mr Pres clears his throat and shuffles from one foot to the other. 'Er, sure we will,' he mumbles. 'But, um, let's just take it one day at a time.'

So until that magical time when Mr Pres is truly free, you'll have to be content with what you can get: stolen moments in the toilets aboard his private jet, furtive gropings in the back of his official car, and working through Mr Pres's favourite book, *101 Uses For A Cigar*. If the worst happens, and news of your affair breaks, you're sure you'll come out of it smelling of roses. I mean, look what happened to that other girl, Monica something, the one with the dark hair... She ended up in *Friends*!

But for now...

YOUR CELEBRITY ADVENTURE IS OVER

38

Brilliant news – you've been asked to write your memoirs!

Who would have thought it? You, Shampayne Sullivan, an actual author! Imagine going into Waterstones and seeing your very own book on the shelves! You try to imagine entering a bookshop. Hmmmm... You try a bit harder... Nah, still can't do it!

It's an exciting project, but you're a bit worried you won't be able to handle the actual writing part of it. The last thing you wrote was a poison pen letter in Year 11 to some girl whose boyfriend you fancied. What's more, your 3-inch gel nails make it impossible to type or hold a pen.

'Please don't worry about that,' the commissioning editor tells you. 'We'll get a ghost writer to do it.'

You're shocked. God, what kind of cowboy publishing company is this, that they can't even afford to employ real, live writers? But then again, if you've got your pick of dead people...

'Could Shakespeare do it?' you ask hopefully.

The commissioning editor snorts with laughter. Shakespeare's obviously a no-no then.

'You're so entertaining, Shampayne!' she says. 'We're so glad to have you on board with this. The book's going to be a huge hit. We're sure you've got lots of fascinating tales to tell.'

'Oh, I have,' you say with a knowing smile. 'I've got lots of juicy secrets to share.'

'Fabulous.' The commissioning editor holds out a pen. 'If you could just sign the contract here... and here...'

It's a struggle, but by gripping the pen in your teeth you manage to put a cross in the right places. And six months later, *Shampayne's Secrets* hits the shelves. You'd have preferred it if they'd gone with the title you suggested, *Shampayne Cock Tales*, but the publishers felt their version had more mass-market appeal.

'I've been on an incredible journey,' the jacket copy reads. 'I started out with nothing, and I've pulled myself up by the brastraps to achieve C-list stardom. Now you can read all about my astonishing rise to fame, including how my celebrity lovers measured up, the female stars I consider the biggest slappers and cows, and how my love for Satan has kept me going during the dark times.

'Packed with all-new, exclusive colour photographs of me with very few clothes on, this book will reveal not only my backside, but a side of me the public rarely gets to see: my *in*side. I will share my most intimate secrets and my deepest thoughts, about everything from nail varnish and vajazzling, to hair straighteners and nail varnish.

'I'm Shampayne Sullivan, and this is my story.'

YOUR CELEBRITY ADVENTURE IS OVER

39

Wow, you can hardly believe it! You've landed a part in *Oakyholes*! It's a hugely popular show, set Somewhere Up North, featuring a load of good-looking teens who somehow go to university at what appears to be a leisure centre at the bottom of their road. The UCAS criteria appears to be possession of one GCSE certificate and two ginormous breasts, so you're going to fit right in.

On the surface *Oakyholes* looks like an ordinary town but it's actually a really dangerous place, with a higher murder rate than downtown Caracas. So you're a bit apprehensive. From what you've seen of the show, your chances of getting shot or stabbed, being forced to engage in incest or underage sex, turning bisexual, carrying out a hit-and-run, commiting suicide or becoming a racist homophobe are pretty high.

Despite your worries, you can't wait to get stuck in to your part. Your character's called Roxy Bitchface, and she's not very nice. She steals Gemma Sweetheart's boyfriend, turns him into a drug addict, sells him into slavery and then breaks into Gemma's house and chops off her arms with a machete. And that's just episode one.

Although you haven't had any acting experience, you clearly impressed the show's producers at your first read-through.

'Wow, there's nothing behind the eyes!' Giles, the director, exclaims in awe, as you mime slashing Gemma's prone body with an imaginary blade. 'They're totally dead. You're a natural, Shampayne!'

In fact, the whole team seem delighted with you. They're asking the writers to expand your part so you feature in more episodes than the five you were originally slated for.

'I think Roxy could really develop as a character,' Giles tells you. 'She's ambitious, cold and conniving, and she wants to be queen bee of Oakyholes. We really think you can do justice to her portrayal.'

There's only one drawback: the words. You thought you'd be able to just make them up as you go along – that's what it sounds like all the other *Oakyholes* characters have been doing all this time. You didn't realise that someone actually writes the words down beforehand and you have to, like, *remember* them.

You wave your script at Carl Potter, the ex-model who plays your boyfriend. 'How the hell do you remember all this?' you ask despairingly.

'It's not easy,' he admits. 'I just say them over and over, and over again, until the words go in.' He taps the side of his head. 'It works eventually.'

That night you try Carl's technique. 'Them, them, them, them, them...' you chant, tapping your head. 'Them, them, them, them...'

Wannabe

The next day, you STILL don't know the words. Carl's technique is rubbish! You can't believe you have to remember this gobbledygook anyway. It's not that important – they're just words.

But clearly the director and the rest of the cast are a bit anal about these things.

'Shampayne, that's your cue!' Giles yells at you exasperatedly. 'You're supposed to say, "Yes, it was me that chopped her up, but you'll never take me alive, copper!"'

'Isn't that what I said?'

'No, it *isn't*!' Giles says, his face almost purple with anger. 'You said, "Hey, did anyone see *Rabbit Rehab* last night?"!'

'Oh, did I?'

'Yes!' Giles sighs. 'Look, Shampayne, this is your last chance. Get on top of your lines, or we'll have to rethink the direction your character is going in.'

The next day, an updated script arrives in your email inbox: you have zero lines. Roxy loses her voicebox after accidentally drinking a tumblerful of acid instead of vodka and tonic, and becomes a vengeful mute, wreaking silent revenge on the other characters with a hedge trimmer. At the end of episode five, Roxy – by now a mass murderer – explodes in a fireball at the garden centre, throwing herself through a window straight into a wood chipper, scattering shoppers with her nubile body parts.

It's a fantastic exit, but you'll be sorry to leave. The cast and crew are like one big happy family.

They arrange a leaving party for you, which is sweet. But would you believe it, they completely forget to tell you! You only find out they're all going for a curry by looking on Twitter. Actors are so flakey! When you turn up at the restaurant, a few hours late, they at least look really embarrassed.

Wannabe

The only seat free is at the end of the table, near the toilets, but that's okay – you're next to Lee King, who plays Roxy's drug-dealing, cross-dressing, sex-addicted older brother. You haven't had many scenes with him but you've certainly noticed him around. He's built like a brick outhouse – he works out on set every day between takes – and he loves to show off his incredible ripped body in fitted vests and tight jeans. The rest of the cast call him 'Snake' or 'Python' rather than Lee, and you can't help but wonder why.

'Hey,' he says shyly, rubbing his hand up and down your thigh under the table. 'How about we get out of here? My flat's just round the corner, it would be great to spend some time alone.'

There's no reason for you to stay. You've had two bites of poppadom with half a teaspoon of mango chutney and you feel uncomfortably full. But a part of you is holding back. Shouldn't there be more to life than this? What would have happened if you'd been born middle class and gone to university? Would life be all loveliness, and cupcakes, and gorgeous, sensitive men holding open doors for you? Is meaningless sex, devoid of affection or emotion, what you really want?

It *is*? Oh, alright then, off you trot...

If you want to read about loveliness and cupcakes, go to 24 on page 104

If you'd rather find out why they call Lee 'The Snake', go to 36 on page 155

40

You and C-Rock – or 'Sham-Rock', as the press are calling you – make a fantastic team.

The public can't seem to get enough of your relationship. Everywhere you go you're followed by scores of paparazzi. The gossip columns are full of news about which nightclubs you've been to, what you're both wearing, where you're going on holiday... Sure, your sex life is still odd with a capital O – you're now having regular threesomes with C-Rock and Barney the Purple Dinosaur – but you're prepared to put up with it all in return for column inches in *Showbiz* magazine.

All the resulting publicity isn't hurting C-Rock's career, either. His new album – *Big Hits*, inspired by you – goes straight in at number 1. And he's certainly not shy about telling the world about his feelings. He's appeared on *The Tonight Show* to declare his love for you, and jumped up and down on the sofa, and on Jimmy Fallon, to prove it.

Wannabe

Another plus is you're looking better than you ever have. Designers are falling over themselves to gift you clothes and accessories, and you've learnt a lot about grooming, US-style. You've lost a stone, you're sleek, preened and as close to Barbie as it's possible to be without Mattel launching a lawsuit.

So why do you feel so hollow and empty inside? There's a huge, gaping void at the heart of you that no amount of handbag shopping and nightclubbing seems to fill. And then you remember what that feeling is: you're bloody starving!

You're exercising twice a day, and ingesting nothing more calorific than bok-choi juice. But you still haven't achieved your goal of being a size −2. You're beginning to think maybe it's just not possible.

It's not like you haven't tried. You start each day with two hours of cardio in C-Rock's home gym, followed by a hike in the hills. Then it's time for breakfast: a cube of pear and a glass of filtered water with a slice of lime. Later in the day you do an hour and a half of Pilates and spend two hours in the pool. So of course, by supper time, you wolf down your mushroom and spinach leaf. Sometimes, to your shame, you pig out on an almond, or allow yourself a couple of sultanas. But those lapses in self-control don't happen very often.

So you just can't understand why you can't shift that final ounce.

Maybe it's time to do what other Hollywood starlets do, and visit top plastic surgeon, Dr Kwak?

'Don't do it, girl, don't mess with nature,' C-Rock begs you.

'If you're plastic I won't wanna date ya.

Shall I tell you what I might prefer?

Have your booty coated in fake fur,

Wannabe

Replace your eyes with ones made out of glass
Have some wadding stuffed inside your ass...'

Maybe it's best not to listen to C-Rock. You and he have very different ideas about what's attractive. Then again, you really don't want to lose him while you've got such a good thing going. What should you do?

If you think plastic surgery is the answer, go to 41 on page 169
If you'd rather not mess with your looks, go to 16 on page 72

41

You've decided: you're *definitely* having plastic surgery. True, you're almost physically perfect already, but this is LA, and there are always tweaks and improvements to be made.

You strip naked and survey yourself from all angles in the mirror, turning your body this way and that so you can check out your butt and boobs.

'Miss Sullivan, do you mind?', hisses the receptionist. 'You're embarrassing the other patients!'

You glance around. The waiting room has filled up now, and there are a couple of heavily Botoxed middle-aged women, and a silver-haired man who looks like his face is made of candle wax, gawping at you, open-mouthed.

'Sorry,' you shrug, as you slip your underwear back on.

A buzzer sounds. 'The doctor will see you now,' the receptionist announces.

You're still putting on your bra as you go through the door to Dr Kwak's consulting room.

Wannabe

It turns out that Dr Kwak is everything you hoped he would be. Immediately you get a good feeling about him. One look at his qualifications on the wall tells you all you need to know – he's trained as an interior designer, a colour therapist, a personal trainer and a crystal healer as well as a doctor, which means he's well-rounded, and hasn't spent his whole career just concentrating on one thing.

And a lot of these so-called doctors try to pull the wool over your eyes: they *say* they're plastic surgeons when they're not actually made of plastic at all. Now, Dr Kwak is *clearly* plastic – at least 50 per cent, you'd estimate.

'I've had Botox, Restylane, blepharosplasty, a butt lift and pectoral implants,' his promotional literature states. 'If I stood too close to a naked flame, I'd probably melt.'

'Welcome, Shampayne,' Dr Kwak says warmly as you settle down into a comfy chair opposite his desk. 'I like to take a holistic approach to surgery, so tell me about yourself. Let me get a feel for who you are.'

You trust this guy. His eyes are big and brown, just like a puppy dog's, and they radiate warmth and sincerity.

'Actually, they *are* a puppy's,' he explains when you point this out. 'I had mine replaced with my Golden Retriever's.'

'That's wonderful!' you exclaim. 'I'm an animal lover, too.'

'Is that so?' Dr Kwak looks intrigued.

'I love fish,' you continue. 'They're my passion.' Dr Kwak leans forward. 'Tell me – are you a Pisces?'

Wow – he's *so* intuitive! 'Yes, I am!'

'I knew it the moment I met you,' Dr Kwak says triumphantly.

'Was it my outfit? Pisceans are very creative,' you suggest. You had to improvise today as you still can't work out how to use your washing machine, and your gold lamé bikini top and pyjama-bottoms combo certainly attracted a few stares on the way here.

'It's your distinctive scent,' he tells you, looking thoughtful. 'It reminds me of my boyhood when I used to clean out my father's fishing dredge.'

There's a deep connection here. Yes, you're happy to put your body in this half-man/half Ken doll's capable hands. But how far should you go? Do you want Kim Kardashian's butt? Scarlett Johansson's boobs? Cameron Diaz's abs? The world, aesthetically speaking, is your oyster.

And oysters are clearly on Dr Kwak's mind when he carries out your surgery. He has managed to incorporate your love of fish into your makeover: he's given you a stunning trout pout, for starters, and your feet now have lemon soles. You don't quite have Kim Kardashian's impressive rear but you have a definite halibutt. Dr Kwak has also removed your hair extensions and given you a red mullet, which you feel is a step too far. But overall, you look brill! It's more than you could have hoped for. Your unusual new look is going to raise eyebrows, even in LA. Who knows what's next for Shampayne Sullivan? Maybe you'll land a part in the remake of *Jaws*? But for now...

YOUR CELEBRITY ADVENTURE IS OVER

42

Fantastic news! You've landed a part in *Game of Nudes*!

This could be your biggest break yet. One of the most successful TV shows in years, it's a multi-stranded fantasy epic set in a far-off medieval kingdom, featuring sword-fighting, magic, political intrigue and nail-biting drama. *And* nudeyness...

You're going to be playing a pair of breasts. For the sake of the plot, they're attached to a handmaiden called Son-Yar, who's in love with Sir Grayhamm, Lord of the Nine Kingdoms. You're a bit panicky at first – you have a hard enough time remembering your address, let alone pages of dialogue – but the producers are quick to reassure you. 'The words are only a small part of the reason people watch the show,' they explain. 'They really are secondary to the nakedness.'

Game of Nudes – wow! You're beyond excited! Shooting starts in a month, and there's so much to do in the meantime. You need to perk up your boobs with some press-ups and pectoral flys so they can hold their own alongside all those other, professional boobs, which are attached to RADA-trained actresses. You want your knockers to really stand out and get noticed.

The week before shooting begins, there's a read-through at the show's production offices in Soho. It seems the whole cast is there, as well as the director, some bad-tempered French guy called Herbert Depervert, who's permanently scowling. He shouts at the actress beside you, who's playing a prostitute's buttocks in episode two, and makes her cry.

The run-through goes well, though – so well that there's talk of expanding your part to include some full-frontal nudity as well. It turns out your breasts are naturals at acting. They can vibrate gently to express happiness, or droop a little to convey pity or sorrow.

It feels wonderful to be a part of a 'proper' drama series, rather than a soap opera or reality show. And it's energising to be around so many talented people. Many of your fellow cast members are classically trained and have years of theatre experience, apart from the actress who plays Lady Brendarr, Sir Grayhamm's wife. 'I was with the RSC for 20 years,' she tells you. What a leap, from car insurance to acting! It just shows it's never too late to change careers.

Your co-stars have been incredibly generous, and you've picked up so many acting tips and techniques from them. 'Just pull a sad face,' Sir Grayhamm tells you, when you have to film his death scene. Yes, you're definitely a serious actress now.

'You might even get a Bafta,' Lady Brendarr enthuses.

Get up after *what*? Honestly, these luvvies do talk rubbish sometimes!

Wannabe

You've just had the best news ever! Better, even, than when you found out KitKats only have 107 calories: Alana Durban has asked to meet you! She's TV's hottest property, the writer and star of multi-award-winning comedy series *Laydeez*, about a bunch of twentysomething friends in LA, and she wants you – little old you! – to play a vapid English model and drug casualty called Jemima. And shooting starts next week!

'There's something about Shampayne's eyes,' Alana reportedly said, when asked why she'd cast you. 'I want her to bring that emptiness, that spiritual blankness, to the part.'

This really is the chance of a lifetime – your opportunity to make it in the States. You can hardly believe it! Just think of it: you, Shampayne, on Rodeo Drive, swanning from one overpriced clothes shop to the next! Mingling with the stars in nightclubs on Sunset Strip! Hollywood is surely where you were meant to be. Sure, there's the fakeness, the backstabbing, the bitching, the game-playing and the sleeping around to deal with... But if you try really hard, you're sure you can stop doing all of that and make a fresh start.

'Tell Alana yes!' you scream excitedly down the phone, when her casting director calls. 'I'll be on the next plane!'

But before you can even think of packing, there's devastating news: Nana Rose has collapsed and been taken to hospital. She's asking for you.

What are you going to do? You can't leave Nana Rose. You and Satan are her world. This is your chance to give back after all those years of sacrifice...

Then again, you're needed on set right away, and if you don't go, someone else will get the part. You *could* just pretend the hospital never called...

Wannabe

If you want to head off to LA as planned, go to 29 on page 127

If you decide to stay home and care for Nana Rose, go to 46 on page 190

43

Just when you're wondering what the hell you're going to do next, you get the call that's going to change your life.

'Do you think you may have been mis-sold payment protection insurance?' asks the Indian man at the other end of the line.

Yes, as a matter of fact you have! And it turns out you can claim it back!

Who knew?

But it turns out that was just the call BEFORE the call that's going to change your life...

The phone rings again.

'Shampayne?' a woman's voice asks.

Hey, that's spooky! How did she know it was you?

'Yes?'

'This is Sarah Farrell from the BBC. How would you like to take part in the new series of *Buffoon Bungalow*?'

What an opportunity! Millions of people tune in to *Buffoon*

Wannabe

Bungalow every week, to watch a bunch of celebrity has-beens, wannabees, pinheads and imbeciles battle it out for the ultimate prize: being crowned Mildly Less Irritating Than Everyone Else.

'I'd love to!' you gasp.

'That's wonderful news!' Sarah gushes. 'I guess we should talk money. What sort of fee did you have in mind?'

You think for a moment. 'I could give you a couple of hundred pounds, it's all I've got right now.'

'No, we would pay *you*, Shampayne.'

Wow! This just gets better!

'Then maybe you could give me £250? That would pay for my car insurance renewal.'

'Of course!' Sarah sounds delighted. 'Okay, that's fantastic. I'll get back to the producer and we'll be in touch soon with a formal offer.'

You're buzzing with excitement when you put the phone down. *Buffoon Bungalow* has always been your favourite programme, and now you're actually going to be a participant! At last, here's your chance to show the world that you're not the dumb bimbo that the media makes you out to be. That you're... you're... you're... Where were you going with this again?

You start thinking about what to pack. The rules in *Buffoon Bungalow* are very strict: you're not allowed any luxury goods, phones or electronic devices, and you have to leave your dignity at home, too. Oh, never mind, you won't be needing that! Maybe just a few thongs, then, and some hair straighteners, eyelash curlers and condoms...

The other important thing is, you've *got* to have a catch-phrase. You're gutted to hear 'Shutuuuuuuup' is already taken, as is, 'Oh my *God*!' That doesn't leave a lot of inanities to choose from.

Wannabe

Shrieking 'No waaaaaay!' or 'Reaaalllly?' whenever anyone says anything could be cute...

Sarah sends you a contract a few days later, along with a list of the other celebrities who'll be taking part. There's some old guy called Lizzard from some eighties heavy metal band, some has-been called Angela who used to read the news, TV chef Antonio Shouti, Randy Leigh, comedian and celebrity drug addict, It Girl Lady Francesca Antique-Sideboard and Someone Called Matt Cardle.

Entering the house is a bit of a shock. The front door handle has been electrified, so whenever a new celebrity touches it, they get hit with 40 volts. The crowd who've gathered to watch find it hilarious, especially when Angela gets knocked over backwards and everyone gets to see her granny pants.

It doesn't happen to you, luckily, as you're so knackered from dragging your suitcase up the front steps that by the time you get to the door, you've only got enough energy left to kick it and shout, 'Somebody open the bloody door!'

It's Randy Leigh who lets you in.

'Wow, Shampayne! Hi, darlin', how you doing?' he exclaims, pulling you into a bear hug. He smells a bit musty, like something you might find stuffed down the back of a sofa. He releases you for a moment and stares deep into your eyes. 'Are you a Pisces? I'm sensing some Piscean energy passing between us here.'

'No *waaaaaaay*! I *am* a Pisces!' you shriek. 'You must be physic or something!'

'I am,' he explains. 'I can feel your spiritual energy, coming off you in waves.' He places his hands in front of your boobs and makes a humming sound.

This guy is *deep*.

Wannabe

Suddenly, he breaks off. 'Come on, come and meet the others,' he says excitedly, bounding ahead of you like an eager puppy.

You're the last-but-one in, and everyone else is already lounging on the squashy sofas in the Enforced Interaction Room, looking pretty relaxed.

'No waaaaaay! Hiya, everyone!' you shriek, waving and jumping up and down as if it's Christmas Day and you're four years old, like the producers have told you to do. 'It's *so* great to meet you all. No *waaaaaay!*'

Everyone gets up to greet you properly. Everyone that is except for Francesca, who's stretched out over one whole sofa, dangling one tanned, ultra-slim leg off the side. She looks at you with a bored expression and half-heartedly makes a peace sign.

Just then, there's a deafening 'bang!' from outside. You all flinch. *What the hell...?*

'Maybe it's the door slamming in the wind?' suggests Angela.

'That weren't no door, lady,' says Lizzard, shaking his grizzled head. 'I was in 'Nam in '72; I know an explosion when I hear one.'

'He means Chelte*nam*, of course,' says Francesca disparagingly. 'He had an estate next door to my dad's.'

'Attention, bungalowmates!' the in-house tannoy announces. 'Due to an unfortunate incident, Someone Called Matt Cardle will not be joining the rest of you. Will the remaining six contestants please make their way to the Buffoon Bungalow Hot Tub Haven?'

Francesca languidly peels herself off the sofa, all long brown limbs and golden hair.

Already you've decided you hate her guts.

'Bungalowmates, for your first task, half of you must pretend to be dogs, while the rest of you will be "owners". Dogs must eat their food from bowls on the floor and sleep in the specially designed baskets next to the toilet area. They will only be fed when their owners say so, and must do their business on the lawned area behind the hot tub.'

'Being a dog? Well, *some people* have a head start!' Francesca cackles, glancing in your direction.

'If the task is completed successfully,' the announcement continues, 'the winning pair of contestants will receive increased air time and more flattering editing.'

Now *that's* worth fighting for. Who will you team up with? No way are you being Francesca's bitch! You can see her making a beeline for Randy.

'Lizzard, why don't you go with Francesca, seeing as you're sort-of neighbours?' you suggest. The rocker nods.

Angela and Antonio have already teamed up, which means you have Randy to yourself.

'We've got to stay in character,' Randy whispers. 'You be the dog, I'll be the owner.'

'No waaaaaaay!' you say. '*I'll* be the owner, *you* be the dog!'

'I can't be, I'm a Muslim this week, and dogs are unclean.'

'Bloody hell, alright then,' you mutter. 'But I'm not pooing in public.'

As you curl up in your basket that night, after doing your business on the rug next to Francesca's bed, you can't decide whether taking part in *Buffoon Bungalow* was the right decision. Sure, it'll raise your profile but is it too demeaning? Does it make you look too desperate? Surely, debasing yourself at the whim of a disembodied voice is like something from some dystopian nightmare, and by taking part, you're perpetuating the myth that all celebrities are fame-hungry, vacuous imbeciles? These might be the kind of thoughts that would be running around your head if you weren't already fast asleep, dreaming about lip gloss.

The best thing about *Buffoon Bungalow* is getting closer to Randy. He's such an amazing, spiritual person. And he's teaching you so much, about chakras, Hindu mythology, Native American shamanism and ley lines. He gives you daily mantras to repeat, such as 'My conscious breath is a doorway into the truth' and 'I am an overflowing cup of love', which you customise with a few 'No waaaaaays!' to make them seem more personal.

He really keeps you grounded.

'You're like my personal gnu,' you tell him.

'It's about learning to love yourself, Shampayne,' he explains. 'I practise self-love every day, sometimes several times every day. But then, I have a very high love drive.'

Yep, *Buffoon Bungalow* would be pretty miserable without Randy. You don't particularly click with Lizzard, Angela or Antonio, and Francesca has made no secret of the fact she dislikes you. In fact, she disappears into the Bitch Box at least three or four times a day, and you know she's in there, slagging you off.

'The soul has no beginning, middle or end, and no waaaay!' you chant whenever you see this happen. 'No waaaaaay! Goodness, love and beauty – these are my truths.'

You're feeling vulnerable, and Randy is your only solace. So it's just a matter of time before you and he connect your two souls in the physical realm.

'Unreleased sexual energy is a source of all the conflict in this world,' Randy explains. 'We need to unite flesh and spirit.'

He's *so* right. So you grab a quickie behind the bins, where there aren't any cameras.

Wannabe

'Did you feel that vibrational Earth energy, Shampayne?' Randy asks, as he zips up his flies. 'For a moment, we were truly at one with Gaia!'

To be honest, you didn't feel any vibrational energy at all. Randy's penis is the size of a wine-bottle cork yet you're really falling for this guy.

Your relationship with him is probably the most intimate you've ever had. Could you make it work in the outside world? *Buffoon Bungalow* is such an intense place; it's nothing like real life. And the tasks are seriously challenging. One day you're forced to do an eighties-style aerobic workout then lick sweat from each other's armpits; the next, you're required to hop around all day like frogs, and shout out, 'Listen to me, for I am a knobhead!' whenever you want to speak. It almost seems like the show's producers are deliberately humiliating you, just to get higher viewing figures.

They wouldn't do that, would they?

Sometimes you feel like you've had enough. You know that if you want to leave, you only have to go through the blue door at the back of the garden. Should you quit? Or stick it out?

If you want to go through the blue door, go to 22 on page 100
If you want to stick it out, go to 32 on page 144

44

You've made it! You're the UK's answer to Angelina Jolie! No longer plain old Shampayne, you're Saint Shammi. Whenever disaster strikes around the world, you jet in, looking serene and beautiful, to hand out tubes of lip balm and bottles of conditioner to the refugees.

You've received countless rewards for your humanitarian work, including the National Union of Hairdressers' Golden Scissors, and the *Brosse d'Honneur* from the Institute of Mascara Manufacturers.

But your success comes at a price.

'Why?' you sometimes wonder in bed when the nightmares come. 'Why must there be such ugliness in the world?' You've seen some appalling sights: split ends, flaking nails, unwaxed top lips... Hairy legs and armpits haunt your dreams. You hear the cries of desperate women, clamouring for free samples of exfoliating body scrub...

At your lowest ebb, you're even tempted to throw in the towel.

Wannabe

Some places, like the West Midlands, are so far beyond your help that it feels like nothing you can do will make a difference. Then you remember your mission statement: 'To bring beauty where there is only ugliness, grooming where there is only despair, and Veet where there is way too much hair', and you gain strength from it.

Helping others is by far the toughest thing you've ever done. Sometimes you forget what's *really* important: you. But that all changes when you get a call from Je Voudrai cosmetics.

'We love the work you've been doing, Shampayne,' their Head of PR tells you. 'You've made beauty accessible to every woman, whether she lives in a rainforest or a shanty town. We think you'd be a fantastic ambassador for the Je Voudrai brand.'

You, little old Shampayne Sullivan? A Je Voudrai ambassador? Je Voudrai contracts are worth millions of dollars, and bring global exposure. Hollywood actresses and supermodels fight tooth and nail for the chance to bag one.

'Count me in!' you exclaim. 'I'll be on the next flight to New York!'

It turns out that Je Voudrai are launching a range of cometics aimed at the world's last remaining untapped market: nuns. Your charity links make you the perfect woman to promote the 'Holy Irresistible' range of natural-look lip balms, concealers and eye pencils. 'Our market research shows that nuns have an underdeveloped sense of entitlement,' the CEO tells you. 'We're hoping you can help us to change all that.'

It's your first-ever advertising contract, and you're nervous. There's a hell of a lot riding on this but the TV commercial turns out even better than you could have hoped.

The first shot is of you, sashaying through a rundown area

of Brownsville, handing out tins of food to some attractive child models who've been bussed in to play orphans.

'Just because I *do* good,' you announce to camera, 'doesn't mean I don't want to *look* good, too. After all, charity begins at home – and that means taking care of *me*!'

You bend down to ruffle an orphan's hair before adding, 'When you're doing the Lord's work, you need make-up that won't let you down. My Holy Irresistible lip gloss lets me do important charity stuff with glamour *and* grace.'

The camera zooms in for a close-up. You clasp your hands together, as if in prayer, 'Because I'm worthy!'

The campaign's a fantastic success. Nuns everywhere, from Sierra Leone to San Salvador, rush to buy Holy Irresistible cosmetics and Je Voudrai offers you a three-year contract.

You've achieved a level of success beyond your wildest dreams. Maybe not beyond that wild dream when you were stranded on a desert island with Ryan Gosling and the entire Italian rugby team, but close enough. You're a Je Voudrai cover girl! Who'd have thought Shampayne Sullivan could come so far on so little?

YOUR CELEBRITY ADVENTURE IS OVER

45

Great news! You've landed your your first bit of acting work. You're going to be in *Babes in the Wood* at the Countryshire Royal Theatre. You and some part-time model called Michaela will be playing the babes, and the tall one out of the Chuckle Brothers is playing the evil Sheriff of Nottingham. This could be your big break!

It turns out that panto is the best thing you ever did, because this is where you meet DIY expert Andy Mann, of ITV makeover show *Help! My House Looks Like Shit!* Andy's gorgeous, and just the way you like your men: huge and muscly, with a builder's bum you could park a rickshaw in. He's playing Robin Hood, and his green tights leave little to the imagination. You spend ages watching him from the wings. You'd love to get to know him better but you're wary: already he's been engaged seven times and he's only twenty-five. Will he break your heart?

It doesn't take long for Andy to notice you but he's too shy to introduce himself outright. Instead, he sends you a naked selfie of him getting out of the shower, with a sweet message: 'Hot 4 u'.

You reply with a shot of your boobs, and, 'Can you handle me?' This could be the start of something special.

Your instincts are proved right, as later that week, after the final dress rehearsal, Andy grabs you by the box office. He kisses you urgently (he tastes of cigarettes and Pot Noodle). Your knees go weak with desire. You haven't felt like this for, oh, a fortnight.

Silently, Andy takes you by the hand and leads you off down the corridor, where the male performers are getting changed. A couple of the Merry Men give you a knowing look.

There's a cleaning cupboard at the end of the corridor with Andy's name on it. He slams the door shut behind you. 'U r one sxci babe, xoxoxo' he says in Txtspeak. Luckily, you can speak it, too. 'DEGT,' you warn him. 'U hav a GF.'

'Whteva,' he says, pulling you into his arms.

And then you're both carried away on a tide of passion, and make magical love on a maxi-pack of toilet rolls.

It's over pdq.

'Thx,' says Andy, pulling up his tights. 'BTW, marry me?'

'Oh, Andy, yes! YES!!' you reply in English. Your heart leaps with happiness. You're engaged to Andy Mann! This is worth *at least* four pages in *Ooh La La!* magazine.

Andy's agent arranges everything. There's an interview with the two of you in the following week's issue, and some gorgeous shots of you wrapped in a cashmere blanket, feeding each other strawberries in front of a roaring fire. Then there's a double-page spread of you wrapped in fire, feeding each other a cashmere blanket in front of some roaring strawberries... There must have been a printing error.

Wannabe

The press and public can't seem to get enough of Andy and Shampayne, or 'Shandy', as they're calling you. Tickets for *Babes in the Wood* sell out in days. Downmarket magazine and daytime TV offers roll in. Everyone seems happy – except you.

The problem is Andy's wandering eye. Even when he's making love to you, he's looking over your shoulder at some other girl – or girls, or girls and a boy – you've brought home. At work, he seems to be paying a lot of attention to Michaela, and she's lapping it up like the cat that got the cream. And he spends a lot of time on his phone, texting – it can't all be work-related.

'He'll never be a one-woman man,' friends would be warning you, if you had any. 'He'll cheat on you, for sure. You should find someone who really values you.'

What's more, Andy doesn't seem at all excited about your forthcoming nuptials. *Ooh La La!* are paying for the whole affair and you can have anything you want.

'Should we have fireworks, or doves released on the lawn?' you ask.

'You choose,' he says, shrugging, his eyes glued to his iPhone.

Who is he texting? you wonder. Could it be another woman?

You get your chance to find out one morning when Andy goes out to a *Help! My House Looks Like Shit!* shoot, and accidentally leaves his phone behind. He's normally so careful to take it with him. You're convinced by now that he's hiding something.

You pick it up and try keying in a passcode, 1124, which you happen to know is the number of women he's slept with. Bingo! You're in. But what now? Should you go ahead and read Andy's messages? It's a big step to take – it's morally wrong, for one thing, as well as an unforgivable invasion of privacy. What should you do?

Wannabe

If you want to read Andy's phone messages, go to 57 on page 232
If you don't think you should stoop so low, you're probably
reading the wrong book. Go and get stuck into *Jane Eyre*.

46

Hospital is really, really boring. You thought it'd be like *Grey's Anatomy*, but most of the doctors are women, or really unattractive, or about seventy years old. And all Nana Rose does is just lie there, motionless, on the bed. What's more, she's a bit disorientated on all the drugs, so she doesn't appear to be listening to anything you're trying to tell her about how you missed the biggest opportunity of your life to be here. You might just as well go and chat to the coffee-vending machine in the corridor.

'Do you think she'll be back to normal soon?' you ask the nurse as she adjusts Nana Rose's drip. The nurse gives you a reassuring smile. 'I'm sure she will. She's just exhausted, that's all. The best thing you can do is keep talking to her.'

You lean over Nana Rose. She looks so frail. 'Oh, Nana,' you whisper, 'you can't leave us yet, Satan needs you!'

The nurse's eyes widen in alarm.

You stroke Nana Rose's hair. You don't want her to die, but

part of you doesn't want her to suffer any more, especially if it means you could still catch a last-minute flight Stateside. But just then there's a rasping sound from the bed. Either Nana Rose is struggling to speak, or her old wind problem has reasserted itself.

'Shampayne...' Nana Rose's voice is a hoarse whisper. 'Shampayne?'

'I'm here, Nana Rose,' you reassure her, squeezing her hand. 'What is it?'

'Come closer...' Nana Rose's eyes are pleading with you. What does she want you to do?

You lean in, so your ear is just inches from her face.

'There's something I need to tell you. Your dad...'

'Yes, Nana?'

'Tommy Sullivan, he isn't your real dad.'

WTF?!!!

You can't believe what you're hearing! It's like the rug has been pulled from under your feet, the ground has opened up beneath you, and everything you've ever known has been swept away in a tsunami of clichés. If Tommy Sullivan isn't your dad, then *who the hell is?*

'It could have been one of three men...' Nana Rose whispers, her breath coming in little gasps. 'Your mum was dating Rich Liszt, the millionaire businessman, and Rich Pickings, the TV gameshow host. And she also had a fling with Rich Fruitcake, who used to be in that band, the Miserable Tuesdays.'

What? So your dad isn't a used-car salesman after all? And it could be any one of these random guys?

You're devastated. Your whole life has been a lie.

'I can't believe it! I *won't* believe it!' you gasp. Tears blinding your eyes, you run out of the room and into the corridor. You're not sure where you're headed – although you reckon you'll probably end up in the cafeteria and have a pain au chocolat and a Fanta – but you just needed to get away. You need time to get your head around this devastating news.

When you return to the ward half an hour later, you get a shock: Nana Rose's bed is empty, she's slipped away.

'She's gone, love,' the nurse says, putting her arm around your shoulders and giving you a reassuring hug.

Gone! Nana Rose! *Nooooo!*

You check your watch. Still time for a mad dash to the airport...

'It's so sad,' you say. 'She was the sweetest old lady, she never hurt anyone who didn't ask for it.'

'No, I mean she's *gone to the loo*!' the nurse reassures you, seeing your stricken face. 'She just got up and walked there, all by herself – what a recovery! She's one tough old lady.'

Well, it's probably good news that Nana Rose is still here. You need to sit down and have a long talk with her, about what really happened 20 years ago, and why she and your mum lied to you.

But for now, you just want to know one thing: Which one of those three Riches is your father?

You've gathered Rich Liszt, Rich Pickings and Rich Fruitcake together in the Library Bar of the Central London Hotel. It's amazing that all three of them agreed to turn up, given that they don't know you and have no idea what all this is about. You guess your email – 'Please come to my book's denouement' – must have intrigued them.

Three possible dads, and you. It's just like *3 Men and a Little Lady*, you think. Except you're not *exactly* a lady. And Rich Pickings is no longer a man, having had a sex change in 2002.

'Well, well, here we all are,' you say, as coolly as you can. Inside, you're incredibly nervous, but you're angry, too. Angry at these three cocksure men, because they slept with your mum and cast her aside like so much rubbish. And angry at your mum and Nana Rose, because they lied to you all these years. And angry at the wallpaper and the fact that it's Tuesday and the way the chair fabric feels against the back of your legs... because you've got PMT.

'I'm sure you're all wondering why I brought you here today...' You scan their faces. Rich Pickings is toying with his long blond hair and looking bored; you hope to God he's not your father. Rich Liszt, on the other hand, looks the more likely candidate. Slim and fair-haired like you, he looks trim and dapper in his three-piece suit. As for Rich Fruitcake... He's too busy bouncing up and down on his pogo stick for you to get a proper look.

'We're all busy men,' Rich Liszt says impatiently. 'You'd better get to the point.'

You look at him accusingly. 'I believe all three of you knew Tracey Wilkins at one point, 20 years ago,' you say icily.

'I'm not sure I've ever heard that name before,' says Rich Pickings defensively.

But you were expecting this. After rifling in your handbag you pull out a photo of your mum. All three men look blank so you rifle in your bag again and pull out another photo of your mum, topless this time.

'Here,' you say, waving the picture under their noses. 'Tracey Wilkins, remember her? You should do! You all went to bed with her.'

Rich Liszt looks suddenly embarrassed. Rich Fruitcake looks confused but you suspect he always does. You pause for a heartbeat before telling them, 'I'm not happy about it, but one of you three is my father.'

'That's not possible!' splutters Rich Liszt. 'I can't have children, I'm infertile.'

Rich Pickings is looking relieved. 'It can't be me, either,' he says. 'Your mum and I dated but it was just for show; I prefer men.'

So that leaves just one person: Rich Fruitcake.

'Then it's you,' you say, pointing at him. '*You're* the one!'

Rich Fruitcake stops pogo-ing for a second. 'I could be your dad, I guess,' he says with a shrug. 'Frankly, it's all a blank after 1988.'

'Daddy, my daddy!' you cry, throwing yourself into his arms and almost knocking him over.

'Woah, easy, girl!' he cries. 'You nearly hurt Banjo!'

'Is that what you call your pogo stick?' you ask. (You'd better humour him.)

'No, Banjo is my pet dragon.' He frowns. 'Don't tell me you can't see him, either?'

Rich Fruitcake is clearly missing a few sultanas, but you don't care. You feel tears start to roll down your cheeks, and you press your head against his patchwork dungarees. It feels so good to be reunited with your real dad! You feel complete, for the first time in your life. This is what was missing – a father's love. Fame was just a substitute. Deep down, you're not a publicity-hungry wannabee, you're just a frightened little girl who wanted her daddy. And you want to tell the world how happy you are, now that you've finally found him. It's a beautiful story!

Now, how much, you wonder, would *Ooh La La!* give you for the exclusive rights?

YOUR CELEBRITY ADVENTURE IS OVER

47

You've decided: you're going to open a free beauty salon in The Countryside, where you grew up.

You want to give something back to the community. Your enterprise will create jobs for local people, and draw in tourists hoping to share a little of the magic that is Shampayne Sullivan.

And let's face it, country folk are in dire need of a makeover. Spend a day or two in the sticks and you'll see sights that will bring tears to your eyes: women who must be size 12–14 at least; people out walking their dogs wearing fleeces and wellies, with *zero make-up*, who look like they couldn't give two hoots about beauty or grooming. That's what years of deprivation and lack of investment have done to the place. One poor woman you saw in Sainsbury's the other day had thread veins for all to see because she hadn't used any concealer; it makes you so angry you could cry.

'The people of The Countryside are in desperate need of help,' your press release reads. 'They're crying out for facial rejuvenation and minor cosmetic procedures. I'm determined to make beauty accessible for everyone, no matter what their age, their gender or their household income.

'I want to do with beauty what Jamie Oliver has done with food, and give below-average-looking or downright minging people the chance to make the most of themselves. A hairpiece, a spray tan, a French manicure... They're small changes, but they can change lives.

'My salon, Shampers Pampers, will offer a variety of treatments completely free of charge. I want to make it accessible to children, too, as they're so often excluded from tanning salons and nail bars. And I'm against any form of age discrimination.'

You're thrilled to be making a difference. It feels wonderful to be able to help these downtrodden people. Soon, they'll be like people from Billericay or Newcastle: brown, waxed, buffed, exfoliated, threaded, depilated and vajazzled.

Your salon is going to start by offering the basic essentials:

Deluxe Facial: A cleanse and throrough exfoliation followed by a destressing facial massage, to leave skin looking radiant and refreshed.

Relaxing Facial: As above, but a Keane CD will play in the background, sending you instantly to sleep.

Shampayne Hot Stones Body Treatment: Heated pebbles are placed on various acupressure points to extract toxins from the body and £££s from the bank balance.

Vajazzle: Decoration of the vaginal area.

Labazzle: Decoration of the labial area.

Anazzle: You get the idea.

Crystal Healing: A rebalancing treatment performed by our therapist, Crystal.

Debbie Healing: A rebalancing treatment performed by our therapist, Debbie.

Shitsu Massage: A soothing massage performed by Debbie's small dogs.

Lymphatic Drainage Massage: An invigorating massage performed by our plumber, Darren.

North Korean Body Contouring: You'll be stripped naked, coated in mud, wrapped in clingfilm and left alone in a darkened room for between one hour and several months.

Spray Tan in Shampayne's three signature shades: Peach Melba, Orange Mivvi and Barbecued Sausage.

The Shampers Pampers' launch is scheduled for a week's time, but before then there's a press conference.

'Aren't you rather insulting the people of The Countryside by suggesting they're not as attractive as their counterparts in, say, London or Liverpool?' a reporter from *The Serious Paper* asks.

'These people need help,' you say earnestly. 'Those of us who live in cities and big towns take certain things for granted: access to tanning salons, clean, fresh water and decent hairdressers. But when you live in a wasteland, they're just a distant dream. Some of these young girls have to walk three or four miles if they want a pedicure.'

'Don't you think this is encouraging young girls to start obsessing about their looks?' someone else asks.

'But if you don't offer beauty services on a local level, you risk young girls doing their own treatments at home,' you reply. 'Think about it: their own highlights, their own French manicures... Our therapists are only just now repairing some of the damage.'

Wannabe

You're passionate about this cause, and the press are clearly seeing another side to you. There are appreciative murmurs from the audience.

'Shampayne, do you have any plans to expand your charity in the future?' a BBC journalist asks.

'Sure. The ideal would be to set up salons in war-torn areas and refugee camps, so women can look their best whatever their circumstances. But that's something we'll look into in the future.'

There's an enthusiastic burst of applause. *Yes*! You think you've won them over. And the headlines are favourable: 'BEAUTY AND THE BEASTS,' trumpets *The Bun*, underneath a picture of you and two lumpen, middle-aged clients. 'SHAMPAYNE SAVES THE COUNTRYSIDE,' announces the *Daily Maul*.

It seems the public have finally taken you to their hearts. Tweets about you hardly ever feature the word 'death' these days! Better still, your philanthropy has brought you to worldwide attention. You're in talks with Oxfam to see if you can coordinate delivery of essential beauty items to disaster zones.

There's only one thing that concerns you: you haven't had a backlash yet. Every other celebrity has had one, so why not you?

If you want to carry on with your charity work, go to 44 on page 183

If you think you need a backlash, go to 3 on page 13

48

It's incredible – you're a mum! Just like that! You can't believe it was so easy. You've no idea why most women moan so much – on and on for months about swollen ankles, varicose veins, feeling tired and sick, blah di blah di blah. Well, you found the whole thing a breeze! True, you did get a bit puffed out climbing the stairs at the adoption agency office, but other than that, you've come through the whole pregnancy thing unscathed. You're still a size zero with a minnie like a drinking straw.

Sister Theodora, the nun in charge of the adoption agency, gives you a stack of baby catalogues to browse through while she takes care of some paperwork. It's going to be hard to choose – they all look pretty much the same. 'I think I want a brown one,' you muse. 'I'm not sure a pink one will suit my autumn look. Its all about earth tones this season.'

'Well, we have plenty of babies of African and Southeast Asian descent,' says Sister Theodora with a smile. 'They are all looking for good homes.'

She pauses, her pen poised above the form she's been filling in.

'Would you consider a child with special needs?' she asks.

'Of course I would!' you say. '*I* have special needs.'

Sister Theodora looks surprised.

'I can't eat a boiled egg unless it's *completely* set, people just don't seem to understand that,' you explain. 'If you make me a cup of tea, you have to stir it anticlockwise or I can't drink it. My decorator painted my bathroom in bubblegum pink and then I changed my mind and made him do it all again in turquoise. Then I changed my mind *again* and made him do it in purple.'

Sister Theodora frowns. 'I wasn't thinking of *those* types of special needs,' she says. 'What I mean is, would you consider adopting a child who is disabled in some way, or requires medical care?'

You pull a face. 'Would it have all its limbs?'

'Not necessarily.'

'Then no, I don't think so.'

You flick through the catalogue again, and land on a page featuring a photo of a smiling, gap-toothed toddler with curly black hair and huge limpid eyes.

'What can you tell me about this one?'

'Ah, that's Angelique,' smiles Sister Theodora. 'She's from Angola. Her mother was just fourteen when she had her, and was too poor to keep her. So now she's looked after by the Sisters.'

She's cute. 'I'll take two,' you say decisively.

Sister Theodora looks puzzled. 'But there is only *one* of her.'

You sigh, exasperated. 'I mean, this is the *kind* of thing I want,' you say, waving your hands irritably over the catalogue. 'Just get me two along those lines – boys or girls, I don't really mind.'

'You plan to adopt *two* children?' Sister Theodora beams. 'Why, that really is very generous of you, Miss Sullivan.'

She takes your hand – without bloody asking! But because she's a nun you don't slap her or anything.

'I know that the celebrity lifestyle has at its heart a great spiritual void,' she says softly. 'Many famous people like yourself are searching for fulfilment, and many never realise that they will never find true happiness in the number of Twitter followers they have, or the latest handbag, or how many times they appear on the cover of gossip magazines.'

She really needs to let go of your hand now – it's been more than 10 seconds.

'What you are doing is a truly amazing thing,' she continues, smiling beatifically. 'You are giving two children the chance to escape poverty and desperation. Thanks to you, they will know a mother's love. I know you will guide them on the right path through life; steer them away from ephemeral, meaningless things and encourage only the good: empathy, compassion and grace.'

You nod. 'Oh yes, yes, absolutely.' To be honest, she lost you at 'spiritual void'.

Sister Theodora releases your hand. 'In that case, I'll push through the paperwork as quickly as possible. If we are lucky, and the authorities don't drag their heels, the children may even be with you in time for Christmas.'

She beams. 'Now, you must have many questions. What would you like to know?'

You think for a moment. 'Can you gift-wrap them?'

The children, Sugar and Hutt – you've named them after your favourite nightclub – arrive on 23 December, encased in Liberty gift-wrap and ribbon just as you'd requested. They look so lovely and Christmassy under the tree.

Your plan had been to leave them until Christmas morning, but you're so excited you rip the paper off right there and then.

'Oh, look!' you shriek. 'Nana Rose, look at them – they're just gorgeous!'

And it's true – they are. Sugar has huge dark eyes, cocoa-coloured skin and a cute little heart-shaped face. Hutt has a chubbier face – but you're sure you can find a plastic surgeon to sort that out – and wild curly black hair that sticks out around his head like a halo.

The children gambol about on the carpet, giggling with delight. They seem pleased to be free of all that Sellotape.

'They're beautiful, Shampayne,' says Nana Rose. 'Like little lambs.'

'They are, aren't they?' you reply, misty-eyed. You've never felt like this before. Having children has made your life complete.

You watch them playing for two, maybe three minutes.

'Could you take them away and give them a sandwich or something?' you ask Nana Rose. You badly need a break. Who'd have thought motherhood could be so exhausting?

'Come on, then, my lovelies,' says Nana Rose, gathering Sugar and Hutt to her enormous fake bosom. The children try their best to cling on. 'Nana Rose is going to look after you.'

'Thanks, Nana,' you call after her, weakly. Hell, being a single mum is tough sometimes. You can only imagine how Octomom manages.

It seems there are a million things to do now you're a parent – first off, you need a nap. Then you're going out for a pedicure and a back massage. And then you've got to make a start on your celebrity guide to motherhood to be published in the spring. You've never even read a book before, let alone written one, but the publishers couldn't wait to sign you up. They figure ordinary women everywhere really need to hear your take on things. When they read about your wall-to-wall nannies, private nurseries and privileged celebrity existence, they'll be inspired to be better mothers.

Although you were anxious about motherhood, Sugar and Hutt are delightful. You haven't bought them a playpen yet so they spend most of the day in Satan's old dog crate in one corner of the kitchen. Usually they're let out for photoshoots and things like that, but most of the time they're content with each other's company. They're not whiny babies at all: Sugar mostly just dribbles and stares through the bars of the crate, while Hutt sleeps 23 hours out of every 24.

It's so wonderful being a mum. You want to give your children everything that you never had: only the best clothes, the best schools, the best plastic surgery. If Sugar doesn't have big boobs when she grows up, you'll buy her some. If Hutt can't get a good-looking girlfriend, you'll buy him one. Money has given you a cushion, a sense of security. You'll never be poor again.

Or at least it seems that way, until a letter comes through your door.

WTF? It's a bill from HM Revenue. Apparently, you owe them £220,000!

You can't believe it! You've never even heard of that nightclub, let alone run up a bill there for such a massive amount…

'It's your *tax* bill, Shampayne,' explains Nana Rose.

'Two hundred grand on taxis!' you splutter. 'There's been some mistake!'

Nana sighs. She looks exhausted whenever you talk to her these days; it must be all that getting up in the night. You'd do it yourself, but by the time you've got dressed, done your hair and put your make-up on, the children have usually cried themselves back to sleep.

Nana Rose waves the bill under your nose. 'You have to pay it, Shampayne, or you'll be declared bankrupt.'

'And what happens then?'

'You basically become Kerry Katona.'

Now that's not good. You need to do everything you can to avoid such a state of affairs.

'You'll have to cut back,' Nana Rose continues. 'How much are you spending on beauty salon appointments? Going out, clothes, make-up, holidays... all those sorts of things?'

Your blood runs cold. You're not giving up your essentials! The taxman can take away your dignity, yes, but your personal trainer, make-up artist, stylist, regular massages, Botox injections and designer-handbag splurges? No way!

There must be *something* you can do. The children are costing you quite a lot – perhaps they could eat a bit less?

'There's big money in showing off your bits and pieces,' Nana Rose suggests. 'Why don't you do one of those nudey magazines, like *Lothario*?'

You think about it for a moment. *Lothario* carries a lot of prestige. Lots of Hollywood actresses and top models have appeared in it without any knickers on. Why not you?

'I'll do it,' you say, 'but it had better be tasteful. After all, I'm a mother now!'

August's issue of *Lothario* features four spreads devoted to you, including close-ups of your back bottom, your foo-foo *and* your funbags. Nana Rose isn't happy.

'I never thought I'd live to see my granddaughter's front bottom plastered over the pages of a magazine,' she storms, 'when she isn't actually on the effin' cover!'

You can't expect Nana Rose to understand. August is *Lothario*'s annual Swimsuit Butt Close-Up Edition, and the cover is always an ass collage. Nonetheless, the *Lothario* shoot has brought you a whole new level of exposure. Offers of more nudey work come flooding in. And so too do the film offers. The producers and casting agents must have seen something in you, some hidden talent that has only been revealed since you flashed your ladyparts.

'I think a trip to LA is on the cards!' you tell Nana Rose excitedly. 'This could be my biggest break yet!'

You've always wanted to make it in the States, and this could be your big chance. But what about the children? They're so young and vulnerable, and only just getting used to being in a new country. It doesn't seem fair to uproot them all over again.

It's a real dilemma. What should you do? Put yourself and your career first, and go to LA? Or stay at home and look after... Hang on, don't go yet! I haven't finished giving you the options!

To catch the next flight Stateside, go to 19 on page 83

49

Being in a girlband is better than you could have imagined – you're told what to do, what to say, how to dress, where to stand... Someone else even does the singing for you, you just have to mime. It's everything you ever dreamt it would be. The only thing that's spoiling it is Carly. You and she aren't speaking at all, except when you're being interviewed for kids' TV or *Pop is Cool!* magazine, when you have to pretend to be the best of friends.

'And what star sign are you, Carly?' asks the *Pop is Cool!* interviewer.

'She's Fido, the Dog,' you jump in.

Carly gives a fake laugh. 'That's why we connect, and we're such good friends,' she smiles. 'Shampayne was born in the Chinese Year of the Slag.'

'Ha-ha-ha-ha,' you laugh, pinching Carly's leg so hard your knuckles turn white. 'We're like sisters!' Carly trills, grinding her stiletto heel onto your big toe.

Still, 'Oooh!' is an instant smash. Your video is on MTV every five minutes; Swedish House Mafia do a special party remix and it's played everywhere from Ibiza nightclubs to school discos. Your follow-up single – 'Aaah!' – is released just two months later, and this time you get five 'Aaahs' and Carly only gets two.

Gideon is delighted, especially at the amount of press coverage you're getting. Your habit of topless shopping is certainly grabbing the attention of the paparazzi.

'I've got a new project in mind for you, Shampayne,' he tells you. 'How would you like to be a judge on *Singin' in the Rainforest*?'

Oh wow, what an amazing opportunity! *Singin' in the Rainforest* is watched by half the UK population, and it's a hit Stateside, too. This would take your profile sky-high.

'I'd love to!' you gush. This could be your biggest break to date!

You and Nana Rose are huge fans of *Singin' in the Rainforest*. It's addictive TV: 12 wannabee West End stars are parachuted into the jungles of Belize, with only basic rations and no medical supplies. Every week they have to battle hunger, illness, deadly insects and tropical storms while learning complex lyrics to Stephen Sondheim show tunes, in order to compete in a Saturday-night sing-off.

You'll be mentoring your team of three via satellite link-up. It's going to be brilliant fun, but incredibly hard work. You've had to practise for three, maybe even four minutes every day, pulling sad faces in the mirror and making it look as if you give a shit. It isn't easy. You're getting better at crying on demand, though. One of the contestants, Gavin, is obese and recently lost his pet hamster. Whenever he appears on screen you just think about the time you broke a nail cleaning out Swimmy's tank, and the tears flow uncontrollably. You've also been learning aphorisms from *The Little Book of Blah*. 'Your dreams are like grapes,' you tell your team. 'If someone crushes them, turn them into wine!'

'What does that even mean?' asks one of your contestants, Michelle, who has the voice of an angel and the sticky-out ears of a Toby jug. God, you hate her!

Of course, you've no idea what it means either, but you've found that if you just smile beatifically and look tearful, and place your hand over your heart when you speak, you can get away with any old rubbish.

'After the show is over, you guys can call me any time, day or night,' you assure your team, 'and I promise you, you'll be connected straight to my voicemail.'

This series of *Singin' in the Rainforest* has the highest viewing figures ever, and after a few weeks, you realise something odd has happened: you've become the nation's sweetheart!

The media seem to love you, too. 'Shammi Sullivan is reminiscent of Lady Di,' claims the *Daily Maul*. 'The Chix singer wears her heart on her sleeve, and struggles to keep her emotions in check.'

The Serious Paper does a two-page feature declaring you to be the representative of a new wave of altruism sweeping through British culture. *The Daily Phworr!* publishes a nip-slip picture of you with the headline, 'WHAM, BAM, THANK YOU, SHAM!'

Meanwhile, Carly and the other girls are seething with jealousy. 'It isn't fair!' they complain to Gideon. 'Why does she get all the attention?'

Gideon shrugs. 'She's simple, people like that.'

The public love you right now, and they'll love you even more if you decide to do some charity work. But what kind of work? It will have to be something that doesn't involve people who smell, sick people, old people or you actually getting your hands dirty...

If you want to launch your own beauty charity, go to 47 on page 195

If you want to adopt a couple of orphans, go to 48 on page 199

50

Your wedding has made the front page of *The Bun*!

There's a gorgeous picture of you and Johnny beneath the headline – 'SHAM MARRIAGE!' – lying passed out, hand in hand, on the lawn outside the marquee.

'Boho bride Shampayne Sullivan tied the knot with indie wildchild Johnny X yesterday at St Stephen's church in Upper Classington, and afterwards partied until dawn at the groom's parents' Gloucestershire vicarage,' you read.

'The groom sported a 1970s velvet suit, while the bride wore a vintage see-through Biba minidress and no bra. Celebrity guests and liggers mingled in the sunshine and enjoyed free champagne, cocaine and publicity.

'Roads around the church were blocked off for the duration of the celebrations, while unattractive villagers were herded into large pens outside the village boundary in case any of them accidentally wandered into shot.

Wannabe

'"I'm sure they all had a lovely time," said ninety-six-year-old Florence Cole, whose cottage lies within the grounds of the groom's parents' 20-acre estate. "It went on until 8am. The music was so loud my dogs were howling, and they refused to come out from under my bed. But I only cried twice, so it could have been worse."'

It's a great write-up. Your official wedding photos will be appearing in *Ooh La La!* next week, so there's going to be blanket coverage. Plus, there's sure to be plenty of pap shots of you and Johnny on honeymoon in the Caribbean.

Life couldn't be better. You've finally made it! Shampayne Sullivan: successful model, rock-star wife. All you need to complete your picture-perfect life is a wife-swapping session with Jude Law and his latest squeeze. Oh, and a baby, probably. You're sure you can get one of those from somewhere. Johnny and you won't be able to have children of your own, unfortunately, owing to his asthenozoospermia. Which is a fancy way of saying his sperm can't be bothered to move.

You're *sooooo* happy! As you watch Doves being released on the lawn to play some of their greatest hits, you cling to Johnny's skinny arm and smile. You just know this marriage is going to last, for at least three to four years. And afterwards, when The Libraryteens have fallen out of favour and been forgotten about, like The Stoned Rosies or Nirnarnia, and your relationship has irretrievably broken down, there'll be another, cooler, more relevant celebrity husband to find.

The best is yet to come. But for now...

YOUR CELEBRITY ADVENTURE IS OVER

51

Of course, that white-chocolate mouse is just the start. It's not long before you're sucked into Dustin's seedy world of sugar consumption.

That's not to say it's not fun at first. Triple Coco Crunchy Crispies, with chocolate milk, makes a much nicer breakfast than Marmite on toast. Why have chicken salad for lunch when you can just have a Mars Bar? And sweets bring you and Dustin closer. You spend hours on the sofa together, watching cartoons and stuffing your faces with jelly worms.

Indeed your hotel suite becomes the ultimate party pad. Dustin's entourage – mostly kids he's met at the park – come over at all hours of the day with cake, and you play pass the parcel or musical bumps for hours. You don't even know the names of most of them – faces come and go – but one boy, Lucas, is probably the wildest of the lot. He's only eleven but already he's had four fillings and one tooth extraction. He doesn't even bother with sweets; he just turns up at the door with a kilo bag of Tate & Lyle and a couple of teaspoons.

'Do you really think you should be taking your sugar neat?' you ask Dustin as he licks some spilt sugar off the coffee table.

'Relax, babe,' he says, pulling you into his arms. 'Why don't you try some?' He dips his finger in the sugar and touches it to your lips. It's crunchy, it's sweet...

'Gimme some more,' you murmur. It's so good, like nothing you've ever tried before.

You're having the time of your life, letting all your cares and responsibilities slide. You forget to clean out Swimmy's tank and he develops fin rot, but you can't even be bothered to take him to the vet.

You don't want the party to ever end, but Dustin's management announce that he's due back in LA in a matter of days.

'I want you to come with me, Shampayne,' he tells you. 'You won't believe the candy you get in the States. We have over 40 flavours of chewing gum – can you imagine that?'

You're excited. You can't wait to try the sweets he's told you about – Milk Duds, Bubble Yum, Tootsie Rolls...

'What about Chix?' Gideon says angrily when you call to let him know. 'You can't just leave the band in the lurch.'

The truth is, you don't care about the band any more, all you care about is having a good time. And life in LA is even more wild than it was in London. People sell sweets openly in kiosks on the streets; girl scouts even come to your door selling cookies. Sugar is everywhere you turn...

But one afternoon, when Dustin's at the recording studio and you're home alone, munching your way through a packet of Jelly Babies, you have an epiphany. No, it's not a chocolate bar, it's sort

Wannabe

of like a revelation. No, that's not a chocolate bar either; you're thinking of Revels...

Anyhow, you open *Showbiz* magazine to see a picture of you stumbling out of a nightclub on Sunset Strip, a rope of liquorice dangling from the corner of your mouth. 'SHAMPAYNE'S A SHAMBLES!' the headline reads. You don't like what you see. Your hair extensions are tangled. Your skin – once so flawless and fake-tanned – looks pale and blotchy, and there are chocolate stains on your jacket. What are you doing to yourself? You can't go on like this; you look terrible! You've got to make some tough decisions. Should you have plastic surgery? Or maybe you should do something drastic, like some exercise?

If you want to get into exercise, go to 34 on page 148
If you'd rather go under the knife, go to 41 on page 169

52

This is breaking your heart. 'Look, Dustin, I love you so much,' you explain, 'but you seem to care more about Dolly Mixtures than you do about me.'

Tearfully, you throw a few things into a suitcase – some Biros, a vase, a sample tin of paint... Somehow, throwing things into suitcases always seems to make you feel better. You chuck in a handful of cotton wool buds and a wok; you're feeling calmer now.

You turn to Dustin. 'I don't think we can go on like this,' you say. 'Either the sweeties go, or I do.'

Dustin looks torn.

'Don't say that, Shampayne!' he protests. 'I love you, I don't want to lose you.'

'Then bin *these*,' I say, shaking a packet of Foam Bananas at him.

His shoulders slump, and he gazes down at the floor. He doesn't look like an international heartthrob any more, he seems more like an embarrassed little boy.

'I'll change!' he mumbles. 'I promise you, Shammi, I'll give up sweets for good.'

'Oh, Dustin, I *know* you can do this,' you murmur, wrapping your arms around him and burying his face in your chest. 'I believe in you.'

For a while, things are great. When Dustin gets a sugar craving he drinks a fruit smoothie, or has a handful of raisins. But everything changes one afternoon, when he gets a call from his six-year-old rapper pal, Lil' Foetus.

'I'm going out with the boys, be back later,' Dustin says, looking excited.

It's good to see him so happy.

'Where are you off to?' you smile.

'We're just going to hang around at the bus stop,' he shrugs. 'Maybe play a bit of knock-and-run, or kick over some dustbins.'

'Okay, have fun,' you say, pecking him on the cheek.

You're busy all afternoon filing your nails, but you make sure room service has Dustin's tea ready by 5pm – it's Fish Dippers, chips and sweetcorn, his favourite. Half an hour later, he's still not home. You try his mobile: straight to voicemail.

'Dustin, your tea's gone cold,' you say anxiously. 'Where *are* you?'

All sorts of horrible thoughts are going through your head right now. There's a particularly gruesome one about a sort of scaly-skinned goat-lizard god eating the entrails of a sheep, but you push that one aside and think about what might have happened to Dustin. Has he been arrested for causing a public nuisance in the park? Fallen off someone's skateboard? Eaten too many chips and been sick?

You try to stay calm. He'll be home soon, you're certain; after all, the sun's going down now and Dustin doesn't particularly like the dark.

But it's 3am when Dustin eventually rolls in, waking you from a fretful sleep. He rolls across the bedroom floor, rolls into the ensuite bathroom, and then rolls back out again.

'Hey, check out my new rollerskates!' he shouts at the top of his voice. 'Aren't they epic?'

'Stop it, you'll wake the other guests!' you hiss angrily. 'And where the hell have you been all this time?'

Dustin's eyes look wild and unfocussed. You feel a sudden stab of anxiety. 'Have you had a pick 'n' mix?' you ask urgently.

'Yeah, baby, I've had a pick 'n' mix...' Dustin sings loudly. He's having another sugar rush. 'Give me them cola bottles, fizzy cola bottles...'

Suddenly, his face goes ashen. He clutches his stomach, saying, 'I think I'm gonna hurl.'

Dustin rolls unsteadily into the bathroom and slams the door behind him.

Tears fill your eyes. You can't deal with this any longer; you're just not strong enough. You've given this boy/man everything, and all he does is take. He took your Mint Aero that you were keeping in the fridge for Saturday night. He took a pound coin from your purse yesterday – for more sweets, most likely. You need someone who supports you, nurtures you, and worships the ground you walk on. You don't want to be some spoilt teenage boy's carer.

You're getting out of here... It's time to move on.

If you want to try a new career direction, go to 47 on page 195
If you want to take The Phone Call That Will Change Your Life, go to 43 on page 176

53

'And the Oscar for Best Actress goes to.... Shampayne Sullivan!'
OMG, it can't be true! But it *is* – Bradley Cooper really has
just called out your name!

'Go on, Shampayne, get up there on stage!' Quentin urges you,
giving you a gentle push. 'You deserve this!'

There are whoops and cheers, as well as enthusiastic applause,
as you make your way towards the stage. You watch your footing
carefully, gathering up the train of your $40,000 vintage Oscar de
la Renta dress, but at the very last second Jennifer Lawrence sticks
her foot out into the aisle. You swerve expertly. Ha! You're too
quick for her! She's obviously still not over the 2013 ceremony and
her little accident, even though you've told her a *million* times,
you had ankle cramp and were just stretching.

You're surrounded by famous faces: Will Smith's in the front row;
you spot Tom Cruise, Tom Hanks, Meryl Streep, all clapping politely...
But all you can focus on is that golden statuette. You know, Quentin's

right – you bloody well *do* deserve this. Every second of *The Donkeys of Mons Ride Again* shoot was torture. The corset practically cut you in half; you had to take out all your hair extensions, and filming took place in *Wales*! On top of that, Daisy, the lead donkey who played the doomed Celeste, took an instant dislike to you. You were trodden on, spat at, pooed on, sneezed on and kicked in the shins. You're never going into Swansea city centre after dark again.

No wonder your performance as tragic prostitute Lysette was so convincing. Okay, so the singing wasn't your strong point – 'The donkeys could have done a better job,' was *Entertainment Now*'s verdict – but Quentin felt you hitting all the wrong notes, 'gave your character credibility'.

He was your biggest supporter on set, especially when you shot your toughest scene – your farewell to Celeste. You had to do lots and lots of looking sad.

'Okay, Shampayne, you know that Celeste is on her way to the knackers' yard tomorrow. Sing as if your heart is breaking,' says Quentin.

'I dreamed a dream that you'd be free,' you warble,

'And in meadows green you'd caper

But time has caught you in its snare,

And soon you'll be glueing paper.

But your hooves will prance again, when your....'

'Stop, stop!' the musical director barks. 'She's bloody well off key!'

'She's supposed to be!' Quentin interjects. 'She's traumatised about what's going to happen to her beloved donkey. And don't forget, Lysette smokes 40 Gauloises a day. I think she's got the tone just right – that roughness, that atonality...' He gives you a thumbs-up. 'Good call, Shampayne.'

With Quentin's support, you're traumatised throughout 'Hooves in Heaven' and 'Empty Stalls and Empty Nosebags', and positively suicidal during the big finale, 'When the Boys Come Marching Home, You'll Get Sugar Lumps'.

And all your pretending has paid off. Here you are, wresting the Oscar from Bradley Cooper's grip and clutching it tightly to your chest.

'OMG!' you shriek. 'No waaaaaaaaay! Thank you *so* much...'

Okay, where's your speech? It was here, just a minute ago, tucked inside your dress. Now it's... *Bloody hell, where's it gone?* No, it's definitely *not there*! Shit – you've no idea what you're going to say now... You were going to thank all the little, unimportant people who worked on the film, like the producer and the art director and your co-stars, but seeing as you never bothered to learn anyone's names, you'd got some runner to write them all down for you. Now people will think you're an ungracious bitch. And that was supposed to be your little secret...

Quick, think! What would Kate Winslet do?

'Boo hoo hoo!' you sob, your shoulders starting to shake. 'It's *such* a surprise! Blub, burble...' You fan yourself with your hands and look at the ceiling to try and stop the tears. No, it's no good, you're just not strong enough... You collapse onto the podium. '*So* grateful.. blurble, blurble, blub... *amazing* cast and crew.... boo hooo hooo!'

Your shoulders are heaving now; you're practically hyperventilating. Yes, you might just get away with it! 'Everyone who worked – sob! – on the film... too many to mention... Golly! Boo hoo, blub!' You give an earsplitting howl, like a wounded animal caught in a beartrap. The emergency medical team descends on you from the wings and helps you onto a stretcher.

'An honour... undeserved.... Oh gosh! Aaiiiieeee! Aaaaargh! Blurble!...'

The audience are on their feet now, whistling and cheering, drowning out your cries. You've just given the performance of a lifetime! You'll probably be hospitalised for weeks – luvvie-itis is currently incurable – but it's been worth it. Farewell, adoring public! For now, at least...

YOUR CELEBRITY ADVENTURE IS OVER

54

This could be your big break! You're about to model for Brandi Lynn's Dirty Panties. Okay, it's not quite so classy as Victoria's Secret, but it's still a best-selling brand, or at least it is at Walmart branches in the Bible Belt.

Only the best-looking D-list celebrities and softcore porn stars are chosen as models. Every spring and fall they host a big show at a Superspeedway circuit in California, and all the top celebrity pervs come to watch.

Already you're in great shape, but Brandi Lynn's Dirty Panties insist on nothing less than perfection. The theme of the fall show is 'Buck Naked Parking-Lot Par-tay!', and there's going to be a lot of skin on show. It's a great honour to be selected as a Brandi-Lynn's Dirty Panties Hot-Tub Hottie, and you don't want to let anyone down.

You work super-hard to tone up. You have liposuction on your tummy, a breast lift, and butt implants inserted, until you're exhausted. But the results are worth all that effort.

Wannabe

The brand's designers are impressed when you visit their HQ for a fitting. So much so that they tell you they'd like you – little old *you*! – to open and close the show.

'It ain't fair!' complains country singer Lulu Maclaine, stepping into a Union-flag thong and nipple-tassel combo. 'Why'd *she* get all the glory?'

'Yeah, she ain't no better'n us,' agrees exotic dancer Shyrelle, whose main claim to fame is that she once gave the guy who cuts Charlie Sheen's lawn a handjob. 'She only got two tattoos,' she whines. 'Everyone knows a Hot-Tub Hottie needs at least five – one for each of her kids.'

But you won't let the haters get to you. You're not petty enough to stoop to their level...

In any case, the best revenge is that the show goes better than you could have hoped. As you strut down the catwalk in your stars-and-stripes peephole bra and crotchless panties, waving a six-pack of beer, the crowd is agog; you can feel every man in the audience mentally undressing you. And every woman in the audience mentally covering you with a tablecloth. But never mind them, they're just well jel!

One pair of eyes, in particular, seem to be locked onto you like heat-seeking missiles. And those eyes belong to – wow! You can hardly believe it! – Grant Bachelor, Hollywood's favourite leading man and international heartthrob.

As you reach the end of the catwalk to do your turn, he flashes you a grin. His teeth dazzle you and you almost topple on your 6-inch heels, but you manage to hold it together. My God, he's handsome! Even better in the flesh than he is on film. You don't know what comes over you, but you blow him a kiss. It's not like you to be so forward.

Grant looks delighted, and gives you a playful wink. You stick your finger in your mouth and pout at him. He points at you, then mimes squeezing a pair of imaginary breasts.

You think he likes you!

You're buzzing with excitement by the time you make it back to the dressing room. Grant Bachelor has noticed *you*! He's Hollywood royalty, a proper A-list star! Not like the deadbeats and losers you've dated in the past. Could this be the start of something beautiful?

Steady, Shampayne, you tell yourself, you mustn't get carried away. You've been hurt too often in the past to give your heart away easily. And Grant Bachelor certainly has a toxic reputation. He's dated a string of stunning women, but none of them has made it anywhere near the aisle. Each one gets cast aside when he meets a younger, even more beautiful model. Surely he'll just treat you the same way?

It's at times like these that you ask yourself: what would Lindsay Lohan do? You think about it for a minute. Hmmm, you'd best not do *that*; there's usually a mandatory prison sentence.

Making decisions is *soooo* hard! Maybe you should see what your horoscope has to say? You do a quick search on your smartphone. 'Pisces: a tall dark stranger will make suggestive gestures to you at a fashion show,' you read. 'Corner him at the after-party and offer to boff his brains out. Now's also a good time to think about updating your kitchen or bathroom.'

Thanks, stars! You can always rely on them to help in a time of crisis. And you should definitely go for it – you know Grant won't be able to resist if you turn on the full Shampayne sparkle.

You throw on a bodycon micro-minidress and fluff up your hair. You look *hot*! You take a quick selfie, then a belfie, then a brelfie (a breast shot – keep up!) to post on your Instagram site, then head out the door. You've gotta feeling that tonight's gonna be a good night. That tonight's gonna be a good night. That tonight's gonna be a good, good night!

Wait a minute, didn't you just say that?

Perhaps you're losing your mind over this guy?

As soon as you arrive at the party, you make a beeline for Grant. He's in the corner of the room, chatting to a willowy blonde in a shimmering gold dress.

'Mind if I cut in?' you murmur, elbowing your way in front of Grant's companion.

'Yes, I do, actually!' the blonde retorts.

Grant frowns. 'Off you trot, Margot,' he says casually, 'there's a good girl.'

The blonde looks shocked. You recognise her now: it's Margot Walsh, Grant's co-star in *My Gay Best Friend*, and the woman he's allegedly been seeing for the past year. She doesn't seem happy.

'Go on, then, Margot,' Grant insists. 'We're finished. Move along.'

The blonde seems momentarily stunned. Then she turns towards you. 'I've got some advice for you, sweetheart,' she says, in a clipped East Coast accent. 'You'd do best to steer clear, this guy has major issues.'

'That doesn't bother me,' you say coolly. 'I don't like majors either.'

She gives a little barking laugh. 'Well, in that case, I'm sure you'll make each other very happy,' she says, with a wry smile. She's handling this with class, you have to admit.

'Go on, then, slapper, bugger off!' you mutter tersely. You turn your back to her and angle your body towards Grant's. He leans

225

in towards you, so you're almost touching. It's so intimate, you can almost feel an electric current running between you. Then you realise that prickling sensation is your Lurex dress statically attaching itself to his polyester slacks.

'I thought you were amazing in your last film,' you breathe.

He looks intrigued. 'Oh, which one?' he asks. 'The one where I'm a gay ice-hockey player, or the one where I play a gay one-legged Gulf-War veteran?'

'I was thinking of the one where you played Judy Garland,' you say. 'You were *so* convincing.'

He looks pleased. 'Yeah, I was, wasn't I? I'm up for an Academy Award for that.' He pauses, and looks deep into your eyes. 'But that's enough about me. What about you?' he asks. 'Tell me all about yourself.'

'I like fish,' you say.

'Fascinating,' Grant murmurs. 'You have everything I look for in a woman. How would you like to be my girlfriend for the next six to nine months?'

OMG, that's certainly a tempting offer! As the girlfriend of Grant Bachelor you'd be whisked from premiere to premiere, enjoy holidays in exotic locations, get to meet Beyoncé and Jay-Z and other A-listers... And yet, there's a risk he might break your heart. Do you really want to go through all that again?

You're going to have to think about it. Which is a pain, as you really hate thinking.

If you want to hook up with Grant Bachelor, international playboy, go to 55 on page 227

If you'd rather see what single life in LA has to offer, go to 8 on page 33

55

At first Grant seems like the perfect boyfriend but you soon come to realise there's something different about him. You just can't put your finger on it. In fact, you can't put your hand, your mouth or any other part of your body on it; Grant won't let you anywhere near his manhood.

'Ooh, get off me!' he shrieks as you attempt to straddle him on the couch at his beautifully designed, tastefully decorated condo. You're aching for this man, why won't he get intimate with you?

An added problem is that whenever it looks like you *might* get down and dirty, Ricardo, Grant's personal nutritionist, has a habit of bursting into the room.

'Oh, excuse little old me!' Ricardo snaps, throwing up his hands at the sight of you pinning Grant down on the Persian carpet. 'I just wanted to let Mr Bachelor know it's time for his meat shake.'

At those words, Grant's eyes light up. Hastily, he removes your hands from his belt buckle and stands up. 'I'll be right with you,

Ricardo,' he says. 'Sorry, honey,' he says, turning to you. 'If I don't let Ricardo administer a meat shake at least once a day, there's hell to pay. You know what a little bitch she can be!'

And it's true, Grant prioritises his meat shakes over everything else. It's all part of his punishing schedule for keeping in shape. He does two sessions of weights and cardio a day and has regular vitamin injections. Then there's the teeth whitening, the oxygen facials, the waxing and the eyebrow threading... He spends more time on his appearance than you do but you have to admit, he looks amazing.

In fact, everyone in LA looks a million dollars, and you've upped your game, too. You take up yoga and Pilates, ballet, Zumba and Krav Maga, and give up wheat, dairy, protein, carbs, fruits and legumes. You look great, and you feel fantastic, too. And you're having the time of your life. It's fun being Grant's girlfriend, hanging off his arm on the red carpet as you attend premieres and glitzy Hollywood parties. And because he is that bit older than you and super-sophisticated, you're learning lots of things from him about art and culture and stuff like that. He's taught you that red wine is better drunk alone, rather than mixed with Diet Coke or Red Bull. That Art Deco was an artistic movement, not a folk singer from the 1960s. And that it IS possible to get out of a car without showing the whole world your nunny.

Work-wise, though, there's not much happening. You've been to plenty of auditions, but you've only been offered bit parts. You're worried your past as a pants model is holding you back.

'You need to take the Shampayne Sullivan brand upmarket,' Grant advises. 'Why don't you set up your own lifestyle website?'

A lifestyle website, based on little old you – that's a fantastic idea! And not in the least egotistical. You'll call it SS.com. It'll contain all the information the modern woman needs to look and feel her best. You can give fashion advice and interiors tips, spew out some cod psychology and banal platitudes, and include all your favourite recipes, from your favourite Sparkling Water Smoothie to your fabulous Cucumber and Fresh Air Casserole.

Women are going to love it. It will be super-relevant to their lives. In particular, you want to share the secrets of how you look so good on the $1 million Grant gives you each month as pocket money. But where to start? Maybe you should outline your philosophy of life? Here goes...

You know, in this journey that I've taken through life, I've learnt so many things. It turns out that giraffes can't swim – at all. I mean, WTF?!? But what I have gained most of all is self-knowledge. I have learnt to let go of bitterness and resentment, and strive to see only the good in everyone. It's not easy, believe me. When I think of how Jennifer Lawrence got the part I wanted in American Hustle, I want to rip my yoga mat to shreds and stuff my Native-American Hopi Healing Ear Candles up her smug arse.

It's at challenging times like these that I used to ask myself: what would Jesus do? But I've stopped looking to others for answers. Now, I think to myself, "What would Shampayne Sullivan do?" Yes, readers, it's been a long, hard road, but I've finally learnt to love and value myself for who I am. Every morning, before my pond-algae smoothie, I look in the mirror and chant: 'OMG, how fabulous am I?' 10 times, then I'm ready to face the day. Then whatever shit life throws at me, I can deal with it. If some two-bit wardrobe assistant asks if she can readjust the hem of my dress, and I'm just not in the mood, I'm strong enough to tell her to fuck herself. Or if my pool boy is five minutes late for work, I feel empowered enough to dock a half day's pay from his wages. See how forceful and effective you can be if you just believe in yourself!

There! You've achieved something truly inspiring for womankind. Now all you need to do is post a few links to sites selling $6,000 T-shirts and you're done.

Your film career will take off eventually, you're sure of it. And in the meantime, SS.com can be your legacy. The only weird thing is that your biggest audience at the moment seems to be Nazi memorabilia collectors; they're visiting your site in their thousands! But then they probably need your makeover tips more than most. Whatever, you've successfully classified yourself, and for now, at least,

YOUR CELEBRITY ADVENTURE IS OVER

56

Honestly, some people will believe anything!

Better go back to 21 on page 93...

57

What the hell? There are messages on here to *16* other women! Where does Andy find the time? 'C u soon sxci,' you read; 'u r so hot'; 'horny 2nite'. And there are hundreds more that can't be repeated in a spoof celebrity autobiography.

The lying, cheating scumbag! How could he do this to you? Your wedding dreams lie in tatters. What are you going to do now?

'Oh, Nana Rose!' you weep down the phone. 'I'm devastated!'

'Is this about Santa again?' Nana Rose asks. 'I thought you were over that!'

'It's not *that*,' you sniff, 'it's Andy. He's been seeing other girls behind my back.'

There's a hissing sound as Nana Rose exhales. 'The cheating bastard! No one upsets my Shampayne and gets away with it!'

'What do you think I should do, Nana?'

'Leave it with me, love,' Nana says menacingly. 'I'll speak to Mad Uncle Freddie. He'll know what to do.'

Wannabe

Mad Uncle Freddie is like the Dr Phil of your family. If anyone's having relationship problems, he seems to know just how to sort it out.

You throw yourself onto the bed and weep bitter tears. Of course you should have realised it before – Andy's nothing but a 16-timing rat! You had your life all mapped out, and now you've got to start over. But somehow you must find the strength to carry on. It's at times like these that you ask yourself the same question: what would Gwyneth Paltrow do?

Then you go and do the exact opposite.

Gwyneth, you reckon, would slip into organic-hemp loungewear, do three hours of Pilates, then enjoy a freshly pressed kale and goji-berry smoothie. So you should pull on a minidress and forget to put on any knickers, head down to the nearest nightclub and get completely wasted!

So that's just what you do. It turns out to be a great call – the next morning the papers are full of pictures of you flashing your pixellated foo-foo as you get out of a cab. It's just the exposure you needed. The next few weeks are frantic, with interviews in *Ooh La La!* and the *Daily Maul* about how you're coping during this difficult time. You're invited onto the lunchtime TV show *Mouthy Birds* to slag Andy off, and there's even talk of launching your own signature scent, Whiff of Shampayne.

Meanwhile, Andy seems to have gone to ground. No one's seen or heard from him in days. Little wonder, he must be pretty mortified by all the bad publicity he's getting. Strange how the police say he left his credit card and phone behind, though…

Vince is delighted by the way things are going. 'I think it's time we moved you up to the next level,' he says. 'What's your singing voice like?'

Wannabe

'Really good,' you tell him. 'I've been told I sound "otherworldly".'

'That's great!' says Vince eagerly. 'You should think about writing some songs and sticking them up on YouTube.'

You'd love to! After all, music is your thirteenth love, after fish, French manicures, Reese's Peanut Butter Cups, snow, sequins, UGG boots, cupcakes, *TOWIE*, Smashbox Lip Plumper, being tickled, autumn, and Nando's Chicken Breast Fillet Wraps. And being a pop star could go hand-in-hand nicely with your acting and celebrity-girlfriend work.

But right now, you've got other things on your mind. Like, why are fish fingers so big when fish are so small? If a baby pig is a piglet, why is a sheeplet called a lamb? And could you be up the duff?

This last one concerns you most of all. If your instincts are right, and your tingling breasts and queasy stomach *do* mean you're pregnant, what does that signify for your showbiz career? You hadn't planned on having a baby right now, when things are on the up!

Your mind's a mess. There's only one thing to do: look at your horoscope.

You turn to page 54 of *Ooh La La!* magazine. 'Pisces,' you read. 'You might feel that family and friends are taking you for granted right now. A lucky break comes by way of a letter with a red stamp. Oh, and do a pregnancy test: in all likelihood you're knocked up!'

What should you do? Is it the right time to have a baby? Or should you launch your pop career?

If you want to have Andy's baby, go to 11 on page 46

If you'd rather concentrate on music, go to 26 on page 111